PAMELA NOTTIN

The

Technique of Bobbin Lace

Completely Revised New Edition

B T Batsford Ltd, London

I appreciate very much the encouragement and help that I receive from my husband, Arthur Johnson, and thank him for his patience and skill in producing the illustrations.

First published 1995
First published in paperback 2001

© Pamela Nottingham 1995

All rights reserved. No part of this publication may be reproduced in any form or by any means, without permission from the Publisher.

Typeset by Goodfellow and Egan Phototypesetting Ltd

and printed in Hong Kong

9 Blenheim Court
Brewery Road
London N7 9NY
A member of the Chrysalis Group plc

A catalogue record for this book is available from the British Library

ISBN 0 7134 8683 X

Contents

Introduction

Twenty years ago, at a time when there was no general instruction book readily available, I agreed to write *The Technique of Bobbin Lace*. Today, with more experience as a teacher and with a greater knowledge of English traditional laces I have had the opportunity to revise it completely. The aim is the same: to provide a selection of patterns with full instructions, arranged progressively, and to offer the inexperienced lacemaker the opportunity to learn at home or to re-inforce and add to knowledge gained from other sources.

The first section has advice on equipment and materials as well as information on how to work the basic stitches. It is sensible to master Torchon lace before working on traditional Bedfordshire and Bucks Point laces. Sixteen patterns in the Torchon section encourage the lacemaker to develop a logical approach and to gain in confidence. These patterns can be worked in coarse or fine thread and have many uses. A knowledge of the stitches in the sampler allows the worker to adapt other patterns in the section.

The third section with traditional Bedfordshire and some Cluny patterns includes edgings, insertions and decorations as well as collars and a mat. Advice is given on pricking interpretation and for the making of a collar pattern. The basic techniques for this lace are explained in detail.

Bucks Point lace is explained through a series of graded patterns. Corners have been prepared for traditional edgings and instruction given for the making of others. A sampler of 'fillings' and explanation of their preparation and execution add to the interest of this delightful lace.

The greatest satisfaction of all comes when an article has been completed. A section on joining lace and mounting has been added, so you can display the results of your work.

Much confusion has arisen because stitches, terms and even the names of laces vary from one area to the next. Here, common terms are used as far as possible and each one is explained clearly in the context of practical lacemaking as it arises. Once understood these terms can be applied to other patterns.

Fifty new patterns are included in this new edition and more than twenty of the original patterns have been retained. All prickings have been re-drawn.

1. Equipment, Preparation and Basic Stitches

Equipment

LACE PILLOWS

Pillows allow the bobbins to lie on a slope in order that the threads remain taut and a good tension is achieved. They vary in size and shape according to the country of origin and the requirement of the lacemaker but all pillows should be very hard in order to support the pins in an upright position. Traditionally, pillows were stuffed with chopped straw but today one can buy polystyrene pillows which are inexpensive and quite adequate for beginners. Polystyrene pillows are usually called 'flat' pillows to differentiate them from other types. However, it is in fact domed (a flat piece of polystyrene would be unsatisfactory). Alternatively one could make a pillow using straw.

To make a rectangular (straw) pillow (Fig. 1) take a piece of plywood approximately 35 cm x 40 cm (14 in x 16 in) and remove the sharp corners with sandpaper. Make a cotton bag the same size as the board, leaving one end open. Slide in the board – it should fit very closely – and stuff one side only with finely chopped straw. It is important to pack the straw tightly to achieve a hard pillow. Oversew the open end. When working, raise the end of the pillow

to give the necessary slope towards the lace maker.

COVER CLOTHS

Cloths are required to cover part of the pillow when working and the whole pillow when it is not in use. Make a cover from plain, dark green or blue lint-free cotton or polycotton that can be removed for laundering. It should be rectangular, hemmed on all sides and at least the width of the pillow, but not necessarily as long.

BOBBINS

Each country has its own style of lace bobbin, all possessing the three qualities needed to make it an efficient tool: a slim neck on which the thread is wound; sufficient weight to keep

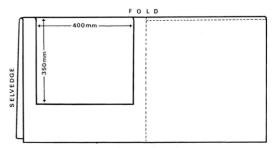

Fig. 1

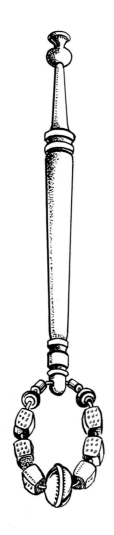

Fig. 2

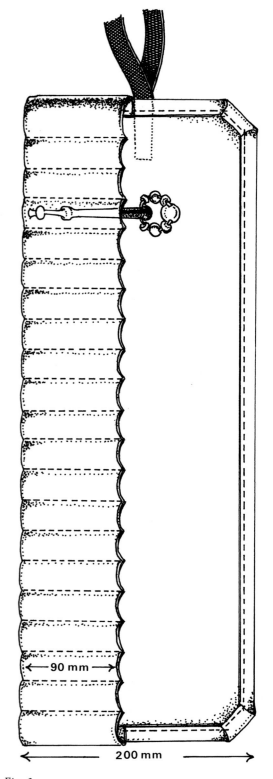

the thread taut to make lace of a clear design and an even tension; and a shape which is easy to handle. Bobbins are made of bone, wood or plastic; some are highly decorated, others are plain and inexpensive. It is essential that the slim North Bucks bobbins are weighted with a ring of beads (Fig. 2). Continental and South Bucks bobbins are not beaded, the weight lying in the thickness of the wood. Always use bobbins of the same type, i.e. South Bucks or beaded.

In order to keep bobbins tidy and ready for use, a bobbin case can be made (Fig. 3). A pair of bobbins can be kept in each compartment and the top folded over for safety. When rolled up it can be fastened with tapes.

90 mm

200 mm

Fig. 3

PINS

Lace pins are made of brass so that they will not rust in the pillow. For patterns in the Torchon section 26/0.65mm pins are recommended. Lace made using fine thread and a pricking with holes closer together requires a thinner pin, 26/0.53mm.

THREAD

Linen thread is the most suitable for lacemaking as it will withstand years of wear and use, however, fine linen thread is no longer manufactured. High-quality cotton is used as a substitute. As bobbin lace is a combination of weaving and twisting threads, a highly twisted thread is unsuitable.

PATTERNS

A well-prepared pattern known as a pricking is essential to achieve lace that is accurate and which has good tension. It is advisable to use a good-quality pricking card (see below) and to mark in guide lines with a permanent ink pen. Other inks or pencil may rub off and discolour the lace.

REQUIREMENTS FOR PRICKING

Pin vice, or pricker. This should have a screw to enable the needle to be replaced when necessary.
Sewing needles: Sharps 8, 9 and 10. For general work no. 8 is satisfactory.
Pricking board: A piece of thick cork or two cork table mats, or a piece of polystyrene.
Drawing pins.
Pricking card. Thick glazed card is essential to hold the pins in position and so achieve accurate lace.

Preparation

TO MAKE THE PRICKING

A copy of the pricking may be made using the photocopier. Alternatively, make a tracing using a pencil with a fine point. Additional advice will be given for Bucks Point and Bedfordshire patterns later.

1 Use a sharp pencil to mark straight lines through ground holes parallel to the footside.
2 Place card, cut to size, on the pricking board, one piece of plain paper over the card and the photocopy on top. Secure with one drawing pin at each corner.
3 Always hold the pricker in a vertical position. Prick one hole at either end of the footside – straight edge – and place a lace pin upright in each. To ensure a straight line, place a ruler against these pins and prick the holes.
4 Place the ruler diagonally across the pattern and prick everything that is truly geometric. The ruler enables the pricker to keep to a straight line and the pencil lines will show up any inaccuracies in the photocopy.
5 Prick in any other holes.
6 Lift the paper, card and copy together and hold it to the light. Check that the pricking is complete.
7 Carefully separate the paper and card and outline the design. Use a pencil and mark with ink when it is correct.

The paper copy can be used for reference. If you need to adapt the design or prepare a corner later, put additional pieces of paper under the pricking. These are more useful than additional photocopies as they can be used in reverse.

TO WIND BOBBINS

When beginning a pattern the bobbins are used in pairs: a knot is never found in lace and so the thread between the bobbins must be free from knots. If the lace thread is on a skein

Fig. 4

it is advisable to wind it on to a spool and then use it from the spool to wind on to bobbins. Hold a bobbin in the left hand and the thread in the right, and wind over and away in a clockwise direction (Fig. 4). Wind evenly as much thread as possible on to this bobbin. Cut the thread. Take a second bobbin in the left hand and wind half of the thread from the first bobbin back on to the second. As soon as the direction of winding has been established it is easier to transfer the bobbin to the right hand, turn the bobbin to wind on the thread which can be guided by the thumb and forefinger of the left hand. Although so much winding seems tedious it is necessary as fine lace thread will twist and tangle if any length is left unwound.

Make a hitch on the thread of each bobbin to prevent unwinding (Fig. 5abc). Allow about 150mm (6in) of thread between the bobbins. Temporarily wind the thread round the neck of one of the bobbins, place in a bobbin case or secure three or four pairs together with a rubber band.

When using bobbins cut from a previous piece of lace, knot them together in pairs, remove the hitch from one bobbin and wind

the thread including the knot back on to this bobbin. Avoid winding back exactly the same amount on each bobbin. Replace the hitch. Instruction will be given later on the removal of knots.

TO PREPARE OR 'DRESS' THE PILLOW

The pattern should be pinned firmly at the four corners on to the pillow. Extra pins along the side are unnecessary and will catch the threads and break them. Allow 5 cm (2 in) of pattern to show and cover the lower part of the pillow with a cloth. This will fit closely if a piece is folded under so that the fold rather than the hem is to the edge. To fasten, use one pin at either side of the pillow. Use a pin cushion or stick pins into the pillow well behind the pricking ready for use.

Additional information

PINS

Avoid touching the thread with your fingers. To facilitate putting in pins, hold the pair of bobbins to the left of the pin in the left hand with the necks well raised. This lifts the threads so that the pin holes can be more easily seen.

Pins at the edges of the lace should slope outwards and, in the centre of the work, slightly backwards.

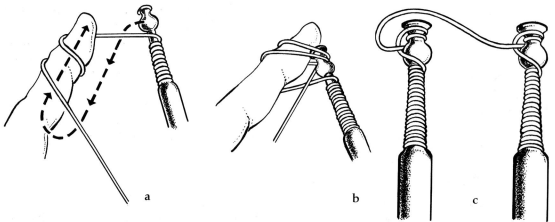

Fig. 5abc

Pins must be kept in the pricking for the complete length on the edges and for two to three inches beyond the working in the centre.

THREADS

The length of the thread between the bobbin and the work should rarely exceed 7cm (3in) in length.

To lengthen a thread hold the bobbin in the right hand horizontally across the pillow. Carefully turn the bobbin towards the worker, at the same time pulling firmly and more thread will be unwound.

To shorten a thread hold the bobbin in the left hand horizontally and with a pin in the right hand loosen the hitch. Keeping the pin through the hitch loop wind the bobbin towards the worker, at the same time pulling to keep the thread taut.

To join broken threads is impossible when the break occurs actually in the lace. Either the lace must be undone until at least 12mm (¹/₂in) of thread is released, or some mending must be done when the lace is removed from the pillow. The latter is not very satisfactory but is carried out as follows. With a clove hitch (Fig. 6), hitch the end of the thread hanging from the bobbin on to a pin, and stick the pin into the pillow close to the back or side of the pricking. Allow the thread to fall into position and continue working. It is successful in a patch of cloth and can, with care, be darned into net, but it is impossible in half stitch.

To join broken threads use a weaver's knot. This is particularly useful when only a short end is hanging from the lace.

Fig. 7a   Fig. 7b

The weaver's knot: Take the new thread and make a slip knot (Fig. 7a). Keep the knot loose. Place the short end from the lace through the loop and pull both slip knot threads sharply (Fig. 7b). If the threads are not joined try again. Trim the ends. The removal of the knot is described below:

To get rid of knots in cloth stitch when the knot is on one of the passive threads, twist the thread with the next thread once and then take it back over the work, loop it round a pin put to the side of the pricking for that purpose and bring it back into work, twist again and continue. If the knot is on the weaver make a faulty stitch to transfer the knot to a passive thread. When work is complete the two ends may be cut close to the lace. *This method may be used in cloth stitch only.*

In all other circumstances pin up another bobbin to the side of the pricking as previously described and allow it to fall alongside the bobbin with the knotted thread. Fasten the two bobbins together with a rubber band and continue using the double thread as one for 25mm (1in) or so depending on the pattern. Discard the bobbin with the knotted thread before the knot is reached. This may be cut off and re-used to get rid of the next knot. When possible it is better to get rid of a knot when it is still several centimetres from the lace.

MOVING LACE ON THE PILLOW

It is necessary to move the lace being made if the piece of work, e.g. a collar, will not fit completely on the pillow. It is also necessary when

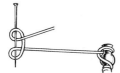

Fig. 6

making an edging with corners, or when working on a flat pillow.

There are two methods of doing this: the first is tedious, requiring considerable patience and skill. In method one, the threads must be pinned to the cover cloth in small groups to avoid confusion later. The cover cloth must be folded up over the bobbins and raised so that it supports completely the weight of the bobbins. Pin it to the pillow. Remove all the pins in the pricking, checking that the cloth fully supports the bobbins and that the threads are not being pulled. Raise the lace and bobbins up the pillow and re-pin in position near the top of the pricking. It is necessary to replace all the pins in several pattern repeats and to pin the edges for a greater distance to the pillow behind the pricking.

In order to move lace by the second method, cut pieces of felt 5 cm (2 in) wide and 75, 65, 50, 40 and 25 mm (3, 2.5, 2, 1.5 and 1 in) long. Arrange these in order on top of each other to form a raised centre and gradual slope at either end. Sew them together, and lay under the lower part of the pattern. Continue to make lace until pins are in the pricking over the centre of the raised part of the felt. The pins will be in the felt and not deeply in the pillow. Support the bobbins as previously described. Remove the pins that are *behind* the felt. Lift the pricking, felt and bobbins to the top of the pillow. Replace more pins as necessary. Refasten the pricking to the pillow and make another pricking that can be pinned below, pattern matching. Continue to make lace and when the felt is free, place it in position for re-use. This method is especially useful on flat pillows and bolsters when working a corner, and it is necessary to turn the lace to continue.

TO JOIN THE THREADS AND CUT OFF BOBBINS

When the lace has been completed it is possible to cut the threads so that the bobbins are taken from the pillow with the threads already knotted together. The method is quickly learned when seen but following written instruction is more difficult.

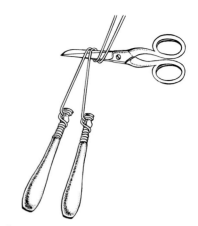

Fig. 8a

Hold a pair of bobbins in the left hand. Take a pair of blunt loose-bladed scissors, hold with the thumb and third finger in normal fashion and place – blades closed – horizontally under the two threads. Twist the thread behind and over (Fig. 8a). Move the pair of scissors through 90 degrees until parallel with the threads and to the right of them. Open the points and grasp the threads above (Fig. 8b). A loose-bladed pair of scissors allows the threads

Fig. 8b

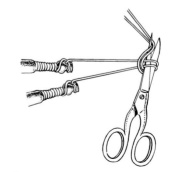

Fig. 8c

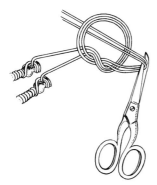

Fig. 8d

to be held (Fig. 8c) without being cut. Pull the blades down through the loop on the scissors, at the same time taking the bobbins in the left hand upwards which helps the loop off the end of the blades. Then cut with the blades (Fig. 8d) and allow one bobbin to fall from the hand, this automatically tightens the knot. Remove one hitch and wind the knot back on to the bobbin, replace the hitch. The knot can be removed during working as described above.

Basic Stitches

Instructions are given for the three basic stitches: cloth stitch, half stitch, and cloth stitch and twist; and the use of the latter to make a narrow beading which demonstrates the method used to obtain the straight edge on one side of a lace edging or both sides of an insertion.

Requirements: Six pairs of bobbins, Bockens linen thread no. 50 or DMC Special Dentelles no. 80.

Refer to Figs. 9 and 10. Prepare pricking 11a.

Prepare the pillow and stick up pins in holes A to F. Hang one pair of bobbins round each pin. The pair hanging at F is known as the weaver – sometimes referred to as the leader or worker. Very temporarily a student may like to mark them with bands or coloured threads wound

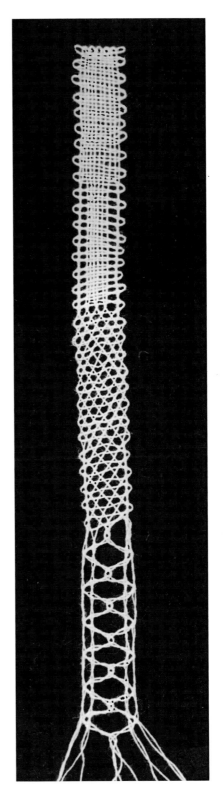

Fig. 9

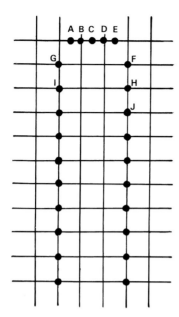

Fig. 10

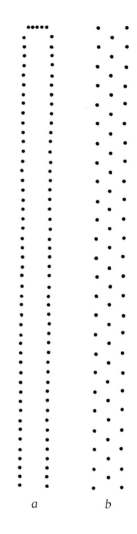

Fig. 11

round the bobbins. Bobbins are always used in pairs and two pairs are used to make a stitch.

Cloth stitch – also known as whole stitch (Fig. 12) Using the pairs hanging from E and F make a cloth stitch as follows. Count the threads from left to right from 1 to 4. The figures refer to the positions only and not to the bobbins so that they must be recounted before each move.

a   Using the left hand lift 2 over 3.
b   Using both hands lift 2 over 1 and 4 over 3 *at the same time.*
c   Using the left hand lift 2 over 3.

The pairs have now changed position, the weaver having passed through the passive pair from E. Discard the right hand pair to the right of the pillow.
   Work another cloth stitch using the weaver and the pair from D. Discard the right hand pair and in turn work cloth stitch with pairs from C, B and A. The weaver is now at the left hand side of the work. Twist the weaver twice by placing the right hand thread over the left and repeating this move. Put in a pin at G to the right of the weaver pair. The weaver is ready to work back to H.

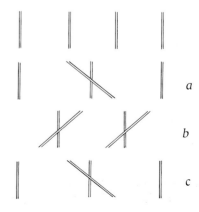

Fig. 12

Work a cloth stitch with the weaver and pair from A. Discard this pair to the left of the pillow. Make a cloth stitch with the weaver and pair from B. Discard to the left and continue. The stitch and twists are always worked with the same basic movements, regardless of the direction of weaving. At the end of each row hold the weaver firmly and 'stroke' the bobbins to improve the tension. Practise until a length can be worked rhythmically and automatically without referring to the instructions.

Cloth stitch and twist – also known as whole stitch and twist This is a variation of cloth stitch and will in this case be used at the edges of the work only. To make the stitch, work a cloth stitch and twist each pair once (Fig. 12abcb).

To continue the practice strip, begin with the pin in position and the weaver at the end of the row. Work cloth stitch and twist with the weaver and first pair. Cloth stitch through the next three pairs, twist the weaver once and cloth stitch and twist the weaver and last pair together. Twist the weaver once more and put in the pin. Continue until it can be worked quickly without referring to instructions.

Half stitch – also known as lattice stitch The weaver changes in every row and only one thread travels across the work. Therefore it is advisable to remove anything used to identify the weaver.

Begin with the pin in position and the weaver at the end of the row. Take the weaver and the first pair and make a half stitch as follows:

a lift 2 over 3
b lift 2 over 1, and 4 over 3, and stop (Fig. 12ab).

These two moves make a half stitch. Discard a pair and using the next pair make another half stitch. Continue across the work and at the end of the row, twist the weaver (i.e. the last pair of which only one thread has actually travelled all the way across) once more. Put up the pin inside this pair as usual. Work several rows, notice that the threads no longer hang straight down singly but are crossed in pairs.

Half stitch is weak at the edges and will become untidy and lose its shape with wear and laundering. Work cloth stitch and twist at the ends of the rows before and after the pin.

Note that cloth stitch and twist is the same as two half stitches.

THE BRAID

Prepare pricking 11b.

Cut the pricking close to the first holes, and cut the pricking on the pillow close to the last row of holes and match them. Pin to the pillow. It is impracticable to try to work through a double thickness of card. Continue with practice stitches until X and Y have been worked, work a cloth stitch and twist after the last pin. Take the two middle pairs and make a cloth stitch and twist. Put up a pin between the pairs at Z. Cover the pin with cloth stitch and twist using the same pairs. The braid will give the worker practice in working the straight edge which is known as the *footside*.

To work the braid (Fig. 13) Work pin A (the footside pin) on the right side of the lace. Take the third pair from the right and work cloth stitch and twist twice to the right to get to the outside edge. Twist the outside pair once more. Put up pin A inside of two pairs (i.e. between the two pairs worked through). Ignore the outer pair, and work cloth stitch and twist to cover the pin. This sequence of stitches is always used on the footside in Torchon lace.

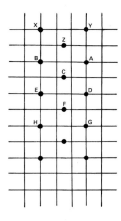

Fig. 13

Work pin B in the same manner. Take the
third pair from the left hand edge and work
cloth stitch and twist twice to get to the outside
edge, and twist the outer pair once more. Put
up pin B inside of two pairs. Ignore the outer
pair and work cloth stitch and twist to cover
the pin. In order to make a working pattern
take the two middle pairs and work cloth stitch
and twist, put up pin C, and cover with cloth
stitch and twist. Take the third pair from the
right and work out as described for pin A in
order to work pin D. Take the third pair from
the left and work out to pin E. Work pin F as
for pin C.

Continue until written instruction is unnecessary.

2. *Torchon Lace*

Torchon lace is the easiest to make, and it gives a student a good general idea of technique. All Torchon patterns are geometric and can be worked out on graph paper. At first a student will copy patterns, but later should be able to make her own quite easily from lace or photographs, or work out her own designs. The patterns described here are progressive and students are recommended to work a pattern until a good understanding is gained before attempting the next.

Explanation of terms used

To cover the pin After putting in the pin make another stitch with the same pairs to enclose the pin. Normally the same stitch will be used before and after the pin.

To hang pairs on a pin Hang pairs of bobbins on the pin so that pairs fall inside each other, thus outside bobbins either side will be the same pair and the two centre bobbins will be the same pair.

To hang pairs on a pin in order As this implies, the pairs will hang side by side, two bobbins of the same pair being next to each other.

The Footside This is the straight edge on to which the fabric is attached. English lace makers work the footside on the right hand side of the lace but Continental lace makers work the footside on the left hand side. A footside is worked both sides when making an insertion. When using a Continental pricking and photograph all that is necessary is to turn them both round and work with the footside on the right.

Torchon footside method has been described fully for the working of the braid. When instructions request that the next footside pin be done it is necessary to work as follows. Take third pair from outside edge and work cloth stitch and twist twice to the edge. Twist the outer pair once more. Pin inside two pairs. Ignore the outer pair, cloth stitch and twist to cover the pin.

The head or heading This is the patterned side of the lace, on the left hand side of the pricking when making lace.

The ground This is the net or mesh and in Torchon lace may be worked in a variety of ways.

Passive threads Those threads which hang straight on the pillow, e.g. the threads which hang down in a patch of cloth, or the pair which lies alongside the footside. Incidentally, when lace needs to be gathered this pair can be pulled to reduce the length of the lace as required.

Direction of working With the exception of passive threads and weavers all the pairs move diagonally in Torchon lace. Pairs enter a patch of cloth or half stitch diagonally, and pairs move diagonally in the ground. In ground, work the hole farthest away first, and move diagonally towards the worker. Normally it is easier to work from the footside as explained in instructions, but there are occasions when it is necessary to work left to right but always from a distant point to a nearer one.

Thread The choice depends on the distance apart of the footside holes. A highly twisted thread, e.g. crochet cotton should be avoided.
  8 squares/25mm grid; Bockens linen no. 35; DMC Coton Perlé no. 12
  10 squares/25mm grid; Bockens linen no. 50; DMC Special Dentelles no. 80
  12 squares/25mm grid; Bockens linen no. 90; DMC Broder Machine no. 30
  Note Patterns in this section are prepared on 10 squares/25mm grid.

FAN PATTERN

Requirements: Eleven pairs of bobbins. Refer to Figs 14 and 15. Prepare pricking 16.

Hang two pairs of bobbins on pin A1, and one pair on each of pins B, C, D, E and F. Hang four pairs on pin G in order from right to left.

To work the ground Using the two pairs hanging from A1, twist the two right hand bobbins three times. Cloth stitch and twist to cover the pin, give one extra twist to the outside (right hand) pair, and discard. Take the inner (left hand) pair and the pair from B, and work cloth stitch and twist but do *not* put up a pin. Discard the right hand pair.

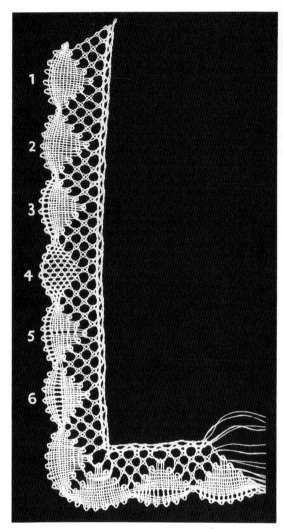

Fig. 14

Take the other pair and pair from C, and make a half stitch. Put up pin 2 in the centre of these pairs, and cover with another half stitch. Discard the right hand pair. Take the other pair, and the pair from D and make a half stitch. Place pin 3 in position in the centre of these pairs, and cover with another half stitch. Discard the right hand pair. Continue using the pair from E for pin 4 and the pair from F for pin 5. Remove support pins B, C, D, E and F.

This is the simplest form of Torchon ground, and in this pattern the rows are always worked diagonally from the footside.

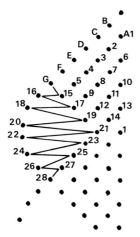

Fig. 15

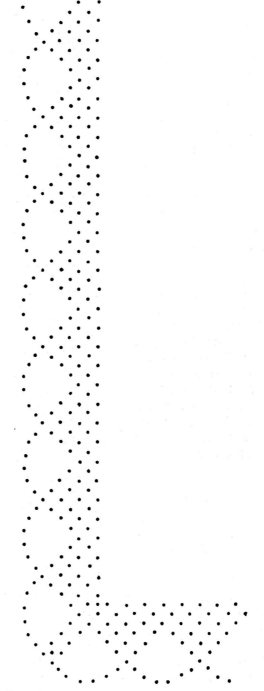

Fig. 16

Work footside pin 6. Using the pair from the footside (i.e. third pair from the edge) and the next pair hanging from 3, work a half stitch; put up pin 7, cover with a half stitch. Discard the right hand pair, and using the pair from 4 work a half stitch, put up pin 8, half stitch. Discard the right hand pair and work pin 9 using the pair from 5. Similarly complete pins 10, 11, 12, 13 and 14. Remember to take the third pair out to complete the footside pins 10 and 13.

The triangle of ground is complete and pairs hang from 5, 9, 12 and 14, and will come into the fan diagonally, one pair at each pin.

To work the fan Begin at G, using the left hand pair as weaver, cloth stitch to the right through the other three pairs hanging on this pin, and through the next pair hanging from 5. Put up pin 15 between these two pairs, and twist the weaver twice. The weaver is the pair to the right of pin 15, and when pulled can be seen to be the pair which has travelled across the work.

Using the weaver pair, work cloth stitch to the left through all pairs. Twist the weaver pair twice, and put up pin 16 to the right of it. Weave back to the right through the four passive pairs and through the pair hanging from 9. Put up pin 17 between the last two pairs; the pair to the right of the pin is the weaver pair and must be twisted twice. Note that the same pair remains as weaver pair throughout the fan. Using the weaver pair work back to the

left through all pairs, twist the weaver pair twice and put up pin 18.

Continue to pin 22 bringing in extra pairs at pins 19 and 21. From pin 22 work back to the right through all the passive fan pairs except one (i.e. through six pairs). Twist the weaver pair twice, put up pin 23 and work back to pin 24. Notice that the pair brought in at pin 21 has been left out after that pin. From pin 24 work back to pin 25 through one passive pair less than the previous row (i.e. through five pairs).

Work back to pin 26 and to pin 27 again through one pair less than in the previous row (i.e. through four pairs). Work back to pin 28, but do not cover it. It is easier to find the weaver pair if it is at the extreme left of the work. Twist pairs hanging from 21, 23, 25 and 27 once each.

Return to the ground Work pin 1 as a normal footside pin, and continue, using the instructions given above, remembering to work diagonally and not to complete the last pin-hole on each diagonal row of ground as it is needed for the fan.

Variations See photograph 4:

1 and 2   Cloth stitch.
3   Cloth stitch and twist on the edge as in the braid.
4   Half stitch with cloth stitch and twist on the outside edge before and after the pin.
5   As fan no. 3, but after pin 21 has been put up, twist the passive pairs once each and continue weaving normally.
6   In the cloth fan the weavers are twisted in the same position in each row, the number of twists arranged to get the desired effect.

Corner (Fig. 17) Complete the pattern as far as the diagonal corner line – indicated by a broken line. Pin y is the corner pin on the footside, and is worked normally using the third pair from the edge – hanging from 14. Pin z is the corner pin to link the fans. Take the fan weavers from pin 28, and weave to the right through the three fan pairs, put up pin z and weave back to the outside edge which will be the beginning of the next fan. Turn the pillow and complete the fan. Study the ground carefully as the footside pin y in the corner has been worked, and the pair from the bottom of the fan and the pair from y will work pin 2.

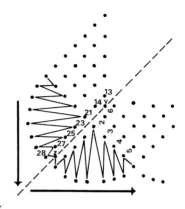

Fig. 17

Complete the diagonal row of ground, pins 3, 4 and 5.

SPIDER AND FAN PATTERN

Requirements: Thirteen pairs of bobbins. Refer to Figs 18 and 19. Prepare pricking 20.

Hang two pairs on A1 and one pair on each of B, C and D, and four pairs on each of E and F in order from right to left.

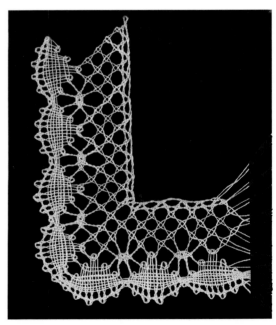

Fig. 18

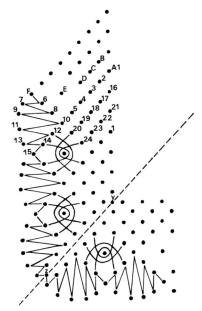

Fig. 19

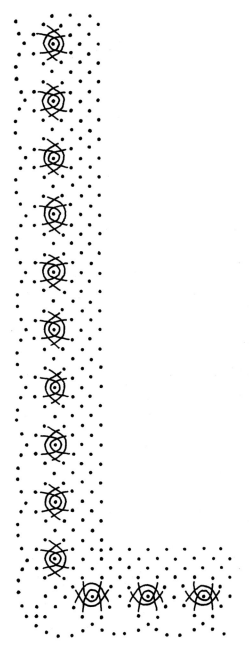

To begin Work the first row of ground from A1
to 5 as in the fan pattern using pairs from E at
pins 4 and 5.

To work the fan The fan is smaller than in the
previous pattern but the principle is the same.
Begin at F using the left hand pair as weaver
pair, work cloth stitch and twist with the first
pair and cloth stitch through the other two
pairs hanging on this pin and through the next
pair hanging from E. Put up pin 6. Complete
the fan bringing in the other pair from E at pin
8 and the pair from 5 at pin 10. Remove support pins B, C, D and E. Remember to twist the
pairs hanging from pins 10, 12 and 14.

To work the ground Work from pins 16 to 24.
Pins 16 and 21 are footside pins worked by
taking the third pair from the edge out to the
edge and the other pins are Torchon ground
worked in half stitch, pin, half stitch.

Fig. 20

Torchon spider (Fig. 21a) The spider is worked
with the four pairs from 14, 12, 20 and 24.
Each of these pairs must be twisted three
times. Each has one twist already and requires
two more. Take the second pair from the left and
weave with cloth stitch through pairs three and

four. Take the first pair and weave through the
next two pairs with cloth stitch. Note that the
pairs have crossed through each other evenly.
Put up a pin between the two centre pairs, and
pull all the pairs to achieve firm twisted legs.
Repeat the movements for the first half of
the spider, i.e., take the second pair from the

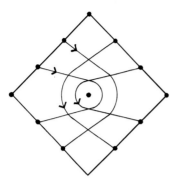

Fig. 21a

left and weave with cloth stitch through pairs three and four; take the first pair and weave through the next two pairs with cloth stitch; twist each pair three times, and pull to improve the tension as the pairs are brought into the pattern. Aim to keep the 'body' flat. A pattern repeat is complete. Work pin 1 as a footside pin and continue.

Corner This is worked in the same way as the corner of the simple fan pattern. Complete the pattern as far as the diagonal corner line, work pins y and z, turn the pillow and continue.

Note that spiders can be worked with many more pairs. Fig. 21b illustrates the spider with three pairs entering on each side. It is worked as follows. Take the third pair (i.e. the left hand pair nearest the centre) and weave with cloth stitch through all three pairs coming from the right. Take the second pair, and weave with cloth stitch through the next three pairs which are those from the right. Notice that the second pair has followed the first but *not* overtaken it. Take the first pair, weave through

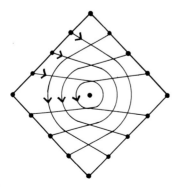

Fig. 21b

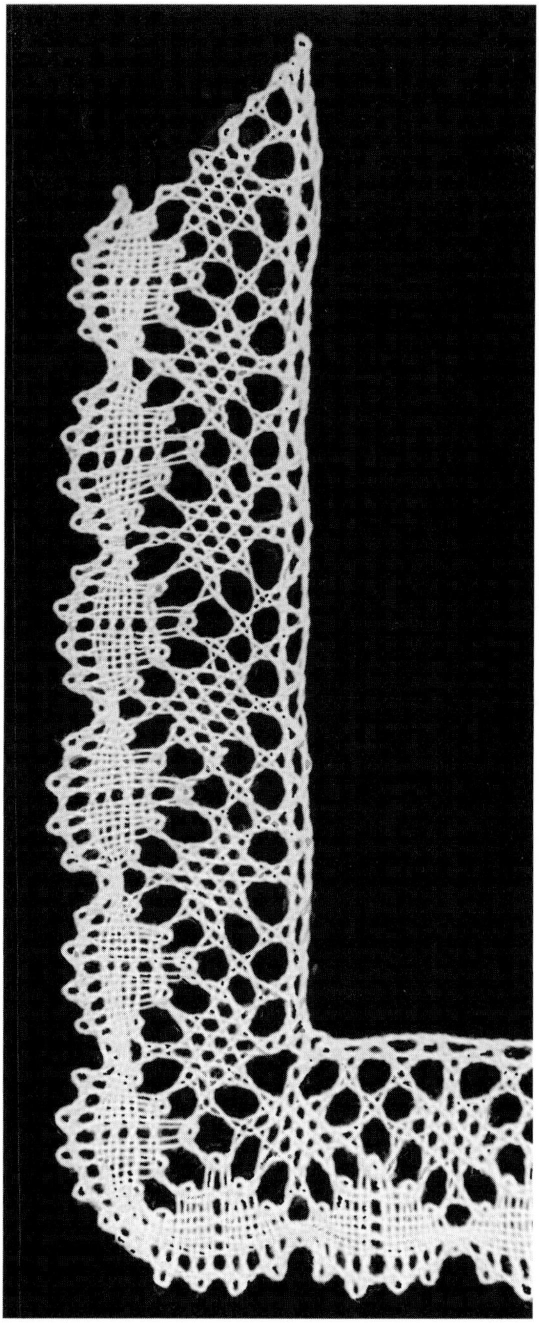

Fig. 22

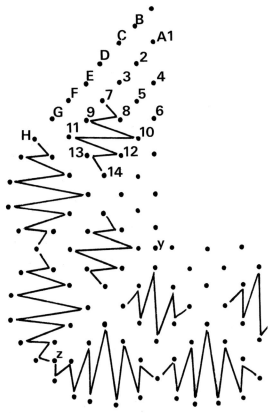

Fig. 23

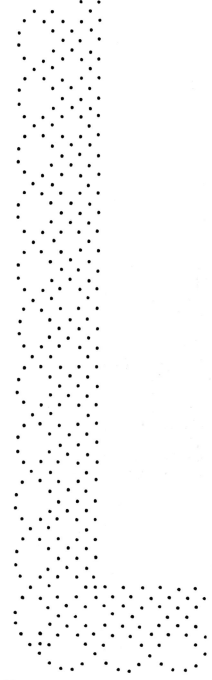

three pairs with cloth stitch, and again notice
that the first pair has followed the other pairs
from the left, but not overtaken, so that they
lie evenly through each other. Put up the pin
between the centre pairs, and repeat the
moves to complete the spider body.

DIAMOND AND FAN PATTERN

Requirements: Twelve pairs of bobbins
Refer to Figs 22 and 23. Prepare pricking
24.

Hang two pairs round A1 and one pair on each
pin B, C, D, E, F and G. Hang four pairs on H.
Work footside and ground to pin 6. Work the
half-stitch diamond starting with pairs from E
and 3, bring in pairs at each pin to the points
at 10 and 11 and leave out as far as 14.
Remember to cover pin 14. Work the fan. Refer
to previous patterns when necessary.

Fig. 24

SPIDER, FAN AND DIAMOND PATTERN

Requirements: Twelve pairs of bobbins
Refer to Figs 25 and 27 and prepare pricking 26.

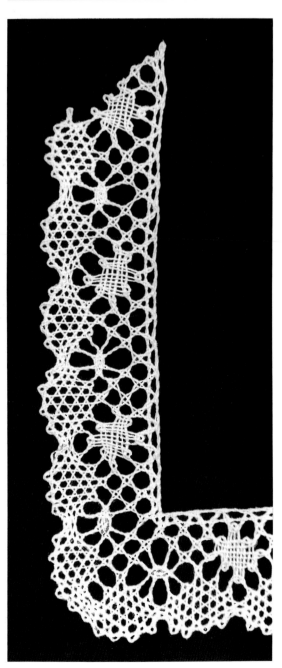

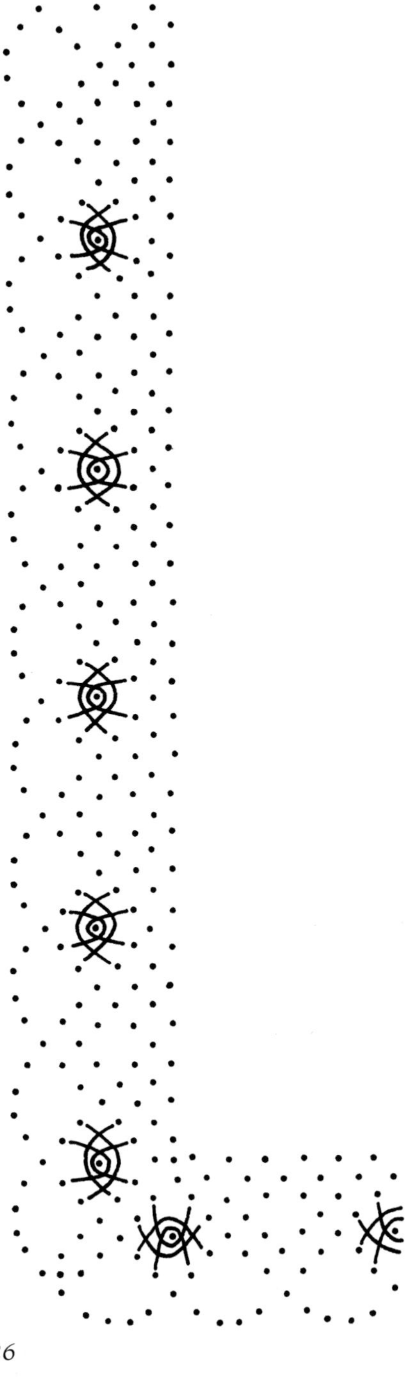

Fig. 26

To begin, follow instructions for the previous
pattern, then refer to the fan and spider pattern.

Fig. 25

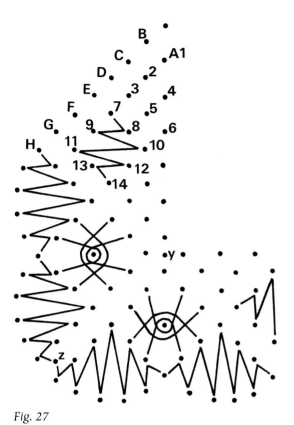

Fig. 27

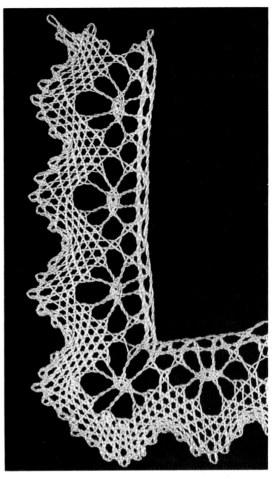

Fig. 28

SPIDER PATTERN

Requirements: Eleven pairs of bobbins and one extra pair for the corner. Refer to Figs 28 and 29. Prepare pricking 30.

Hang two pairs on A1, four pairs on each of B and C in order from right to left, and one pair on D.

To begin Work pins A1 and 2 using pairs as required from B.

To work the half stitch edge This is worked completely in half stitch with the exception of cloth stitch and twist before and after the pins on the outside (left side) edge. Take the pair from D as weaver pair, and work through all the pairs hanging from C, and one pair hanging from B. Put up pin 3 to the left of the weaver pair. Take the weaver pair back through all five pairs to the outside edge and pin 4. Remove support pin C. Weave back

through the five pairs in the half stitch trail, and through one more pair hanging from B. Put up pin 5. Work to pin 6 through the six pairs in the trail, and back through these pairs and the pair from 2 to pin 7. Remove support pin B. Continue the half stitch trail leaving out pairs after pins 7, 9 and 11, as was done in the fan, as far as pin 14. Do not cover this pin, as it will be easier to find the weaver pair at the extreme left side of the work.

To work footside and ground Work pins 15, 16 and 17.

To work the spider Use pairs from 11, 9, 16 and 17, and complete the spider around pin 18. Remember the twists on the legs, before and after the body.

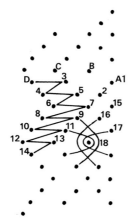

Fig. 29

Order of working Patterns are usually worked
in sections for ease of understanding and
speed of working. It should be noticed that a
complete pattern of trail is worked at one time,
and then pins 15, 16 and 17, which release the
pairs for the right hand side of the spider.
When the spider has been worked, pins 1 and
2 must be worked to lead again into the trail.

Corner (Fig. 31) Work the spider before the
corner and begin the trail in the usual manner,
stopping when pin 8 is in position.

From the diagram it can be seen that the
pairs for the spider's legs hang from different
pins and to avoid a weak trail an extra pair is
joined in after pin 8. Take the extra pair and
put one bobbin under the weaver pair, bring
the loop up and round the pin allowing the
pair to fall inside and to the right of one thread
of the half stitch trail (Fig. 32).

The spider cannot be worked with the usual
pairs as only one pair is available on the right
hand side. The pair from y is not used. All four
pairs must be found before the diagonal corner
line is reached after the half stitch trail has
been worked to this position also (pin 16).

Half stitch trail There are more pins on the outside than the inside edge and to achieve an
even result the pin-holes 13, 18 and 20 must
be used twice. On the second occasion the
weaver pair is put round the pin already in
position. At first, work the trail as far as pin 16.

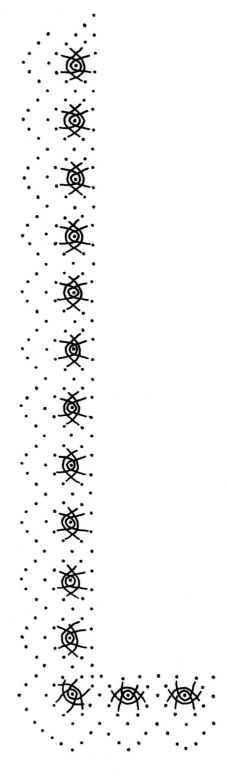

Fig. 30

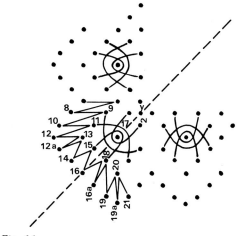

Fig. 31

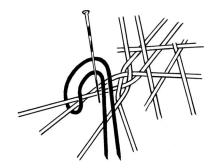

Fig. 32

Remember that pin 13 is the top point and nothing is left out at this pin.

Spider This is worked with pairs from 15, 11, 9 and 17. When it is complete turn the pillow and complete the half stitch trail as far as 21. Use the right hand side leg of the spider and the third pair from the footside corner pin to work half stitch pin 2, half stitch.

The corner is complete and normal working can proceed. To remove the extra pair take the weaver pair at 21, and cloth stitch and twist through the first two pairs of the trail. Take the two centre threads of the four worked through, tie them together in a reef knot, and turn them back over the work. Cross the other two threads and they will lie as the outside passive pair. Later the threads put back over the work may be cut off or for extra strength darned into the half stitch trail.

ROSE GROUND PATTERN

Requirements: Twenty-four pairs of bobbins. Refer to Figs 33 and 34. Prepare pricking 35.

Hang two pairs on A1 and one pair on each of pins B, C, D, F, G, H and J and three pairs on pin E.

The footside Work pins A1 and 2 and the next footpin 3.

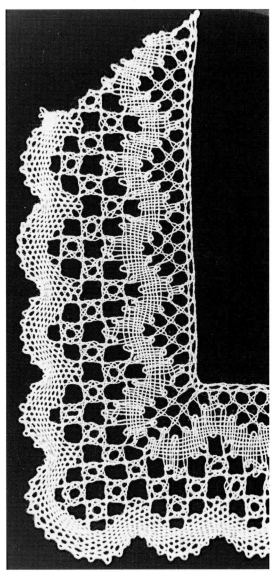

Fig. 33

Fig. 34

The cloth stitch trail Pairs from 2 and D work cloth stitch, put pin 4 between the pairs. Twist the right hand pair twice and weave to the left through the other pair and the three pairs from E. Put pin 5 to the right of the weaver and twist the weaver twice; remove pin D and ease the weaver into position. Weave back through

Fig. 35

these four pairs and the pair from the footside at 3. Put up pin 6 to the left of the weaver, twist the weaver twice and cover the pin. Weave back to the left through one pair only, put up pin 7 and cover. Continue to the left through three trail pairs and one from F. Put up pin 8 to the right of the weaver – the weaver is always twisted as it passes around the pin – weave back through four pairs to pin 9. Put up pin 9 to the left of the weaver, weave back through the trail pairs and one extra from G. Put up pin 10 and continue to pin 14. Twist pairs left out after pins 6, 7, 9 and 11 once each.

The footside and ground Work from 15 to 24. The pair from pin 6 works out to the footside pin 15.

The trail Continue, cover pin 14 and weave to the right through one pair only, put up pin 25 and cover. Continue to the right through the three trail pairs and one from 18; put up pin 26 and continue the trail to pin 6. Twist pairs leaving the trail once each. Hang one pair on each of K and L.

Rose ground This is worked in units of four pins (Fig. 36). Select the four pairs that enter diagonally for unit R and isolate them on the pillow. Pairs from K and L and from 14 and 25 work cloth stitch and twist at a and b. The centre pairs work half stitch, pin c, half stitch. Left hand pairs work half stitch, pin d, half stitch and the right hand pairs work half stitch, pin e, half stitch. Centre pairs complete the diamond with half stitch, pin f, half stitch. The left hand pairs work cloth stitch and twist at g and the right hand pairs work cloth stitch and twist at h. *Note* that there are no pins at the ringed letters a, b, g and h.
   Work rose ground unit S. Pairs from the left already have the cloth stitch and twist (at h)

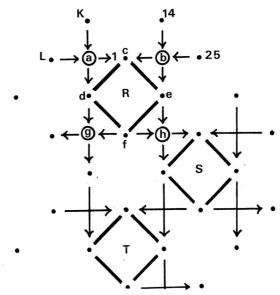

Fig. 36

but those from the right require the stitch to be worked at this stage.

The outer trail Work in half stitch as in the previous pattern. Hang nine pairs on M and one weaver pair on N. Weave through the pairs from M and one from unit R. Continue to n. Work units T and U. Continue the inner trail to o, twist pairs before working the ground.

The corner Work the ground to corner pin p. Complete the inner trail at q. Work units V and W and the outer half stitch trail to r. Work units X and Y and the outer trail to s, leaving out pairs for unit Z. Turn the pillow and work the three units from Z towards the corner pin. Work the outer trail to t, the rose ground unit and the inner trail to u. Ground stitches v, w, and x are worked to the footside. Continue.

CIRCULAR EDGING

Requirements: Twenty-two pairs of bobbins
Refer to Fig. 37. Prepare pricking 38.

For easy matching, the same row of dots is shown at either side of the pricking. It is made in a similar manner to the previous pattern, except that the cloth stitch trail is narrower.

Fig. 37

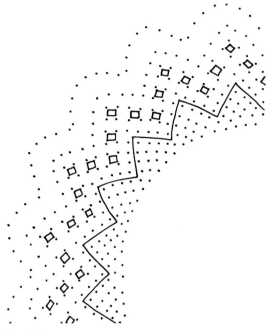

Fig. 38

THE TORCHON CLOTH STITCH AND
TWIST FAN PATTERN

Requirements: Sixteen pairs of bobbins.
Refer to Figs 39 and 40 and prepare
pricking 41.

Hang two pairs of bobbins on A1 and one pair
on each of B, C, D, E, F and G.

The footside and ground Work normally until
six footside pins are in position.

The cloth stitch feature Hang one pair on H
and five in order on J. Work the trail from pin a
to pin b, bringing in one pair from J at each of
the left side pins. Make spider c and complete
the cloth stitch at d. Twist pairs from b to d
once each.

Fig. 39

The fan Hang two pairs on 1 and cover with
cloth and twist. Using the right hand pair as
weaver work through five pairs with cloth and
twist. Put pin 2 between the last pairs worked.
Take the right hand pair to the left through all
(six) pairs to pin 3 with cloth stitch and twist.
Return to pin 4 through five pairs and follow
the diagram to pin 11. Note that one pair is
left hanging out after each even numbered
pin. The weaver remains the same throughout.
Continue the fan, twisting the weaver twice
on all stitches between pins 11 and 13.

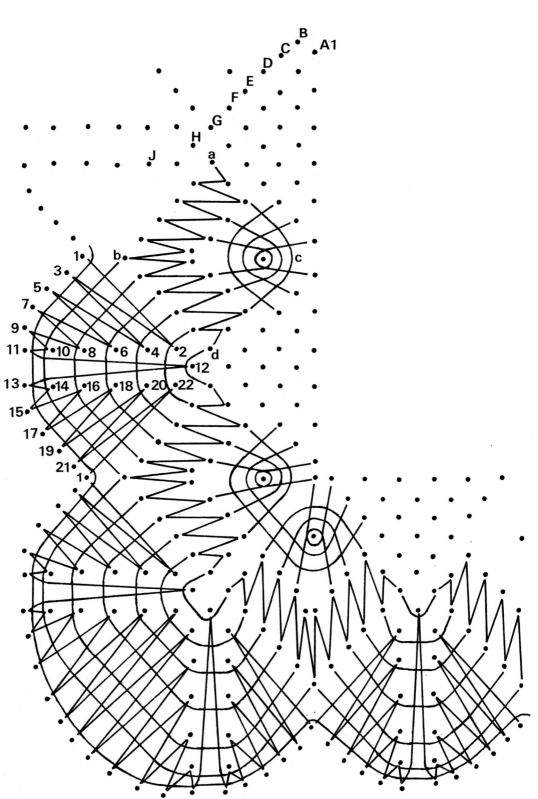

Fig. 40

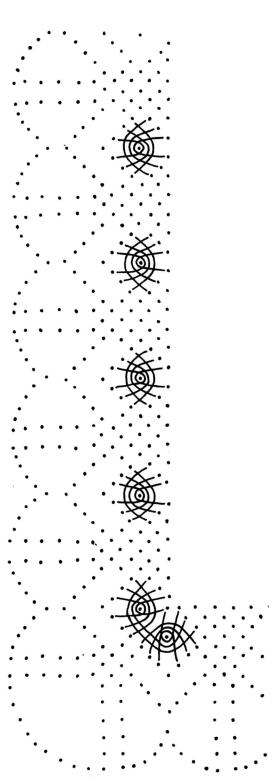

Fig. 41

Complete the other half of the fan, one pair is brought in at each even numbered pin, work to pin 1.

Continue to work in order: ground, half of the cloth feature, spider, complete cloth feature and fan.

To work the corner follow the diagram.

To make Torchon patterns from lace

As soon as the method of making Torchon lace is fully understood, and when the various stitches and their execution are recognized, the making of patterns is straightforward. Torchon lace is worked at an angle of 45 degrees from the footside, and can be worked out on normal graph paper. At first it may be easier to plot the holes on paper with a large grid as it will be easier to see, and then transfer it to the required finer grid afterwards.

To plot the pricking on graph paper (Fig. 42) Grids for Torchon lace can be found on page 182. Mark alternate intersections along a straight line for the footside. Count the number of ground stitches on the longest diagonal row and mark the intersections on graph paper. Add dots for the obvious features – diamonds, spiders and other distinct shapes. Fill in the ground: a ruler will facilitate this. Rose ground appears as squares in the lace, but as diamonds on the pricking. If appropriate a curved line is drawn on the head and small lines marked across it for the pinholes. If misplaced it is easier to erase lines than dots and re-mark until a satisfactory result is obtained. The position of the weaver should be marked to confirm the arrangement. If one curve is accurate, the others may be pricked using a tracing or clear acetate sheet with the holes pricked from the original. Remember that the only occasions when dots are not on a diagonal are as follows: headside curves, centre of a spider, the dots for holes within cloth or for raised spots.

Pricking 43 will confirm the accuracy of your work and if necessary the working diagram (Fig. 44) will assist understanding.

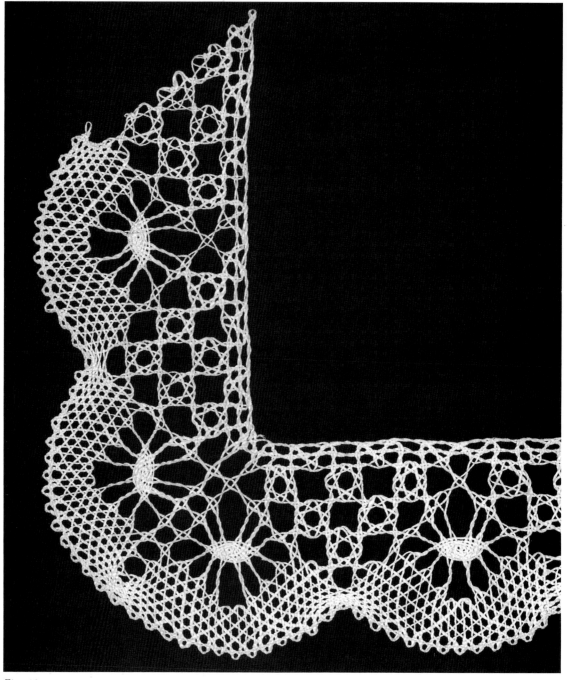

Fig. 42

To plan the corner Take a small mirror with a straight unframed edge and, holding it vertically, move it at an angle of 45 degrees from the footside along the lace until an attractive corner is seen. With a knowledge of Torchon patterns one can decide if it is possible to work it in a straightforward manner. For practice, place a mirror on the patterns given earlier and note where the corner line was taken and how the corner was achieved.

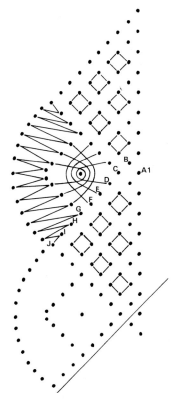

Fig. 43

In most patterns it is possible to have a complete pattern unit before the corner and this
will be repeated afterwards. There are always
two rows of holes, one before and one after the
diagonal corner line – *never* one row on the
actual diagonal. Working the last row before
the diagonal corner line the threads are travelling out and down to the head. When the pillow has been turned it will be found that
threads travel down and towards the footside.
An extra pin-hole is always needed for neatness and goes in the corner on the footside. No
hole will fall in that position because holes are
either side but not on the diagonal. The usual
method for working this hole (usually referred
to as Y) has been explained in instructions for
earlier patterns. A patch of cloth or half stitch
cannot extend over the corner diagonal as the
pillow is turned and the direction of working is
changed. If there is a complete break through
the pattern at the corner it is usual to add
extra pin-holes as required to achieve a neat

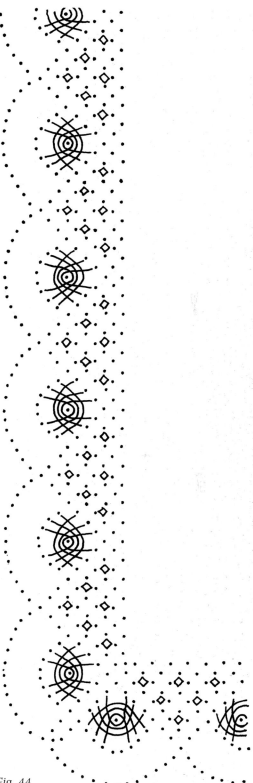

Fig. 44

arrangement of threads on the heading. If there is a continuous half stitch trail the pin holes are used twice when necessary.

Patterns with asymmetric designs require some adaptation. Prepare the corner and arrange to reverse the pattern centrally between the corners. A mirror held at right angles to the footside will show a suitable position. This is illustrated in the reversal pattern (Fig. 47).

To begin working a pattern

To estimate the number of pairs required For a Torchon pricking choose the longest diagonal row of holes, allow three pairs for the footside pin hole and one for each of the others. If there is a cloth or half stitch fan or similar pattern feature extra pairs will be required, usually one weaver pair and sufficient passives to make attractive lace.

SPIDER, ROSE GROUND AND HALF STITCH PATTERN

To begin making the lace:
    Refer to Figs 42, 43 and 44.
    This frequently puzzles the inexperienced worker but is quite simple once a basic understanding of the working of lace has been gained.

1   Decide on the diagonal row of ground that is to be worked first. When possible choose a row that leads into the beginning of a patch of cloth, or half stitch, or a spider. Put up the footside pin A1 on this row, and hang two pairs on this pin, twist the right hand threads three times and make a cloth stitch and twist round the pin. This forms a closely twisted loop around the pin and eventually threads may be pulled through and knotted off if a complete edging is required.
    The two pairs hanging from this pin would normally be the footside pairs with the pin put up inside them but on this occasion the pin has to hold them in position for a firm

start to the row.

2   In Torchon ground, pairs enter the ground and work ground stitches diagonally. A row of support pins may be placed on the row behind the row to be worked, and one pair of bobbins hung on each of these pins B to I. In reality the threads would hang from these pins had the lace already been worked.

3   In a diamond of cloth it is obvious that a pair will come in diagonally for each hole. On the heading when working a pattern with a trail, a fan, or other shape, the pairs will enter one to each hole on the right hand side and the curve on the left hand side will contain all the pairs. By experience or by trial the worker has to estimate the number of pairs required to fill up the edging satisfactorily. It is quite usual to try this out, and adjust the number of pairs required as the effect can be seen. These pairs are hung up on a pin at J, and to achieve a flat heading they are hung in order.

EDGING FOR OVAL MAT

Requirements: DMC Broder Machine no. 30. To use Bockens linen no. 50 enlarge the pricking – 125% using a photocopier. Refer to Fig. 45. Prepare pricking 46.

This is similar to the previous pattern. Refer to instructions above if necessary.

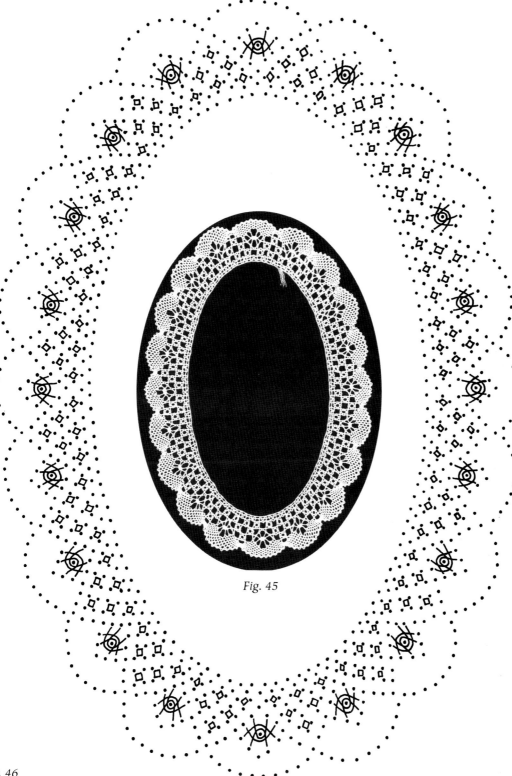

Fig. 45

Fig. 46

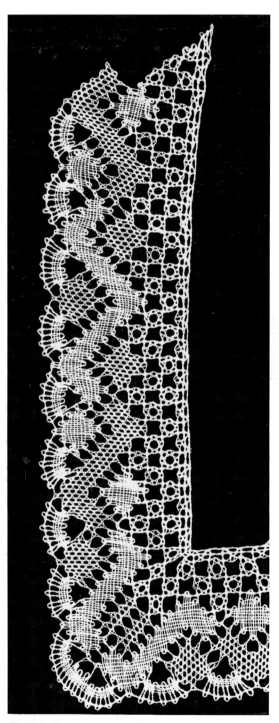

Fig. 47

SCALLOPED HEAD REVERSAL PATTERN

Requirements: Twenty pairs of bobbins. Refer to Figs 47, 48a and 48b. Prepare pricking 49.

Detailed working of the scallop is shown in the diagram. The pairs from d become the weaver and work in cloth stitch through pairs from c and b and through the pair from a in cloth stitch and twist. The weaver has to be twisted on the outward journey to achieve an even result. The corner working is similar although pairs come from the cloth trail. The pillow is turned and the next cloth trail is started at x.

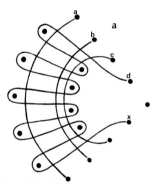

Fig. 48a

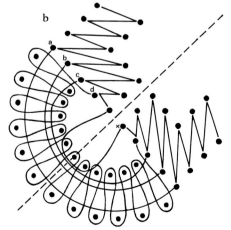

Fig. 48b

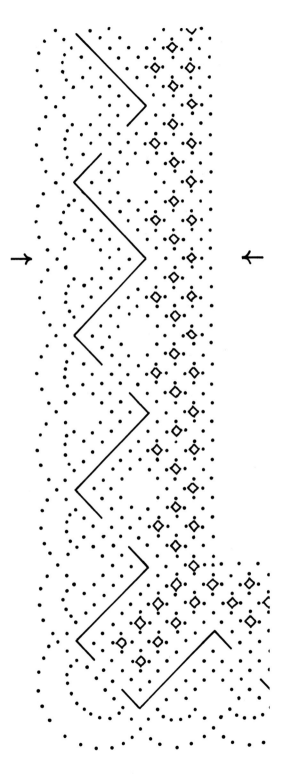

SQUARE MATS

Refer to Figs 50 and 51.

These are straightforward to work and when understood are easy to design. A mat is worked in four triangular sections. Section 1 is worked with the head on the left hand side as

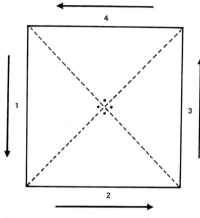

Fig. 50

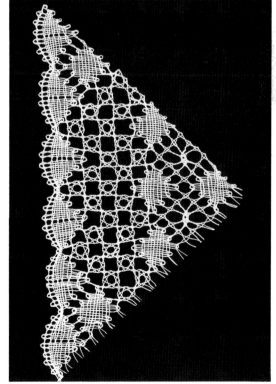

Fig. 49

Fig. 51

usual. When every pin has been put up the pillow is turned as for a corner, and the next section is worked. Again turning the pillow, sections 3 and 4 are worked in turn.

To work the mat

Requirements: Twenty-six pairs of bobbins. Refer to Figs 51 and 52. Prepare pricking 53.

To mark in the rose ground and the weaver and spiders, turn the pattern for each section.

Hang four pairs on the top pin of fan a in order from right to left, and one pair on each of the other pins in the previous diagonal row. With experience the worker will hang pairs on support pins as required as threads waiting for use become twisted and out of position.

The fan Work the fan using the left hand side pair as weaver, the outside edge will be more attractive when the cloth stitch and twist variation is used. Work cloth diamond b and fan c. Work eight units of rose ground d and then fan e. Continue working diagonally, in letter order

Fig. 53

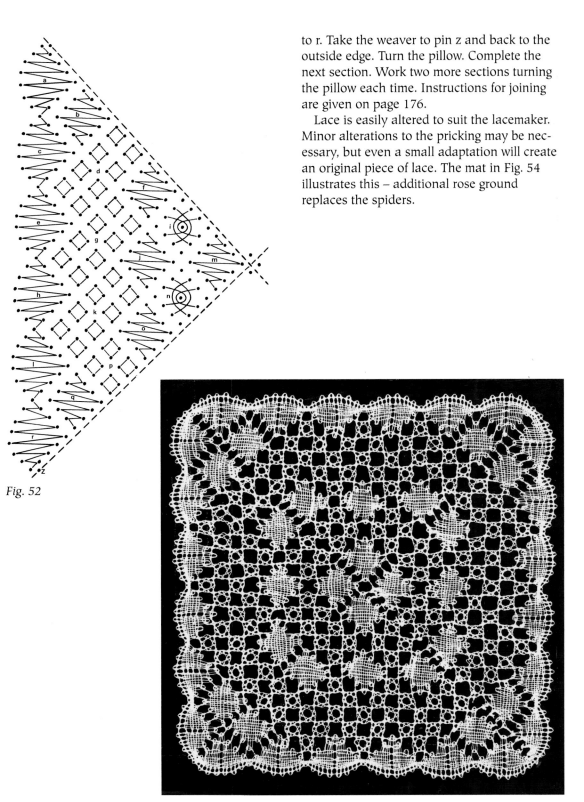

to r. Take the weaver to pin z and back to the outside edge. Turn the pillow. Complete the next section. Work two more sections turning the pillow each time. Instructions for joining are given on page 176.

Lace is easily altered to suit the lacemaker. Minor alterations to the pricking may be necessary, but even a small adaptation will create an original piece of lace. The mat in Fig. 54 illustrates this – additional rose ground replaces the spiders.

Fig. 52

Fig. 54

THE SAMPLER

This is an insertion with footside edge on both sides, it also has neat ends, useful when there is no fabric to mask the edge of the lace. If made as a bookmark the beginning and ending illustrated on page 44 can be used.

Requirements: Twenty pairs of bobbins and one gimp pair, Coton Perle no. 5 or similar thick thread. Refer to Fig. 55. Prepare pricking 56.

To begin (Figs 57a and 57b) To support pairs introduced into the cloth diamond holes are required at the top of the pricking card. The exact position is unimportant as the pins will be removed and threads pulled down into the lace. Hang two pairs on a support pin and work cloth stitch, pin a, cloth stitch. Remove support pins. Hang nine pairs on each side. Work the cloth diamond to pin c, introducing one pair at each pin and two pairs at the points b and c. Hold the weaver firmly and remove support pins to ease the threads into position. Twist all pairs once. Complete the diamond to z, leaving out two pairs after b and c and one pair after the other pins. The pair from d works the footside pin e, continue to ground pin f and footside pin g.

To work the triangle Use pairs coming diagonally to work half stitch, pin 1, half stitch. The right hand pair weaves through the pair from g, put up pin 2 and weave to the left through two passive pairs and one from the diamond. Put up pin 3 and weave back through two pairs only to pin 4. Note that the other pair must be released to work footside pin 6. Work back to pin 5. Work the footside. Weave back from pin 5 through three passive pairs in the triangle and the pair from 6, put up pin 7. Work to pins 8, 9 and 10. Work footside pin 11 with the pair left out after pin 7. Continue leaving pairs out after the apex of the triangle. Cloth stitch may be used as an attractive variation. Pairs for the gimp enclosed diamonds come directly from the triangles.

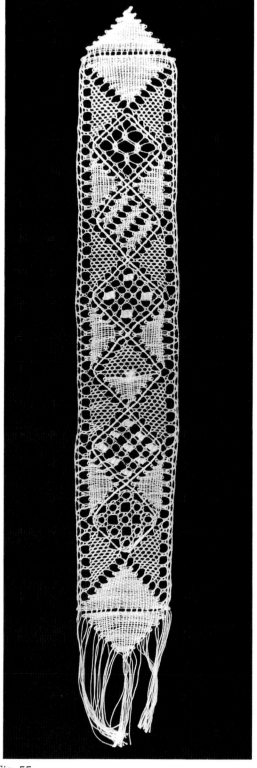

Fig. 55

Gimp threads These outline parts of a pattern. They pass between the threads of a pair of bobbins. In Torchon lace place two twists on the pair before and after the gimp has passed through. When moving the gimp thread it always passes under the left thread and over the right thread of the pair. To introduce the gimp thread in this pattern, support it on a pin at n. Take the gimp out to left and right through six pairs on each side.

PATTERN VARIATIONS

Linked spiders (Figs 57b and c) Remove pin n and work half stitch, pin n, half stitch. Continue the ground holes on either side within the gimp area using pairs from the triangles.

Work spider o. Using pairs from the side of the diamond and pairs from spider o work spider p. Work q similarly. Pairs from p and q work spider r. Complete the sides of the diamond.

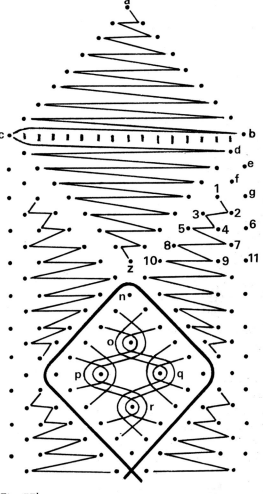

Fig. 57b

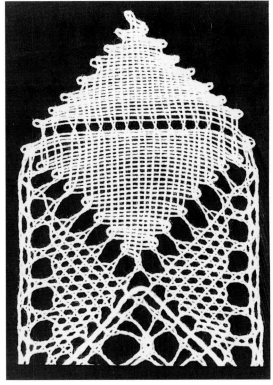

Fig. 57a

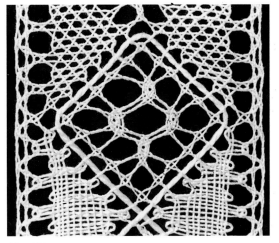

Fig. 57c

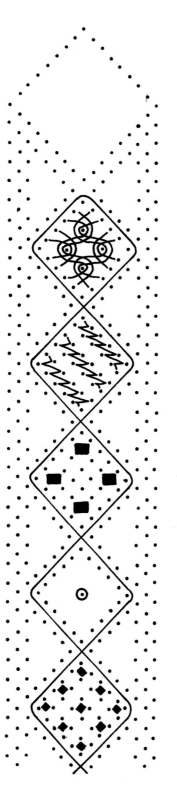

Cloth stitch bars (Figs 58a and 58b) This consists of three strips of cloth, the black lines indicating the path of the weaver. Complete each strip before starting the next.

Tallies, square leaves or spots in Torchon ground (Figs 59a and 59b) From a, work a complete row of Torchon ground in each direction. Take pairs hanging from b and c to make the tally (Fig. 60a). Twist each pair once more so that there are two twists on each pair.

Take the second bobbin of the four as weaver, and pass it over the third as if beginning a cloth stitch. Take it under the fourth bobbin and back over the top of it. Now pass it under the middle thread and over the left hand side thread. Continue weaving in this way so as to get back to the right hand side. To help the threads into shape it is essential to hold the weaver all the time, and, at the end of each to and fro weaving, the outside straight threads must be kept taut and the shape achieved by carefully pulling on the weaver. These tallies require much practice. They are easier to manage in thick thread.

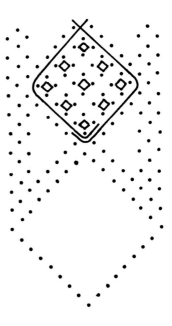

Fig. 56

Fig. 56

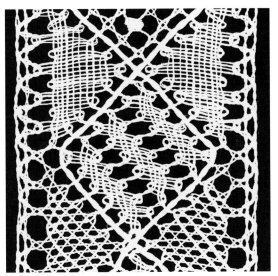

Fig. 58a

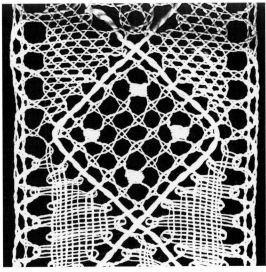

Fig. 59a

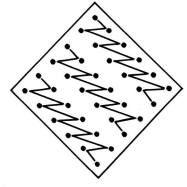

Fig. 58b

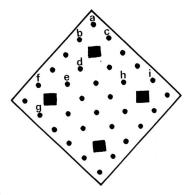

Fig. 59b

At the end of the tally the two pairs are twisted twice each before continuing with the Torchon ground. It is important to work in the pair without the tally weaver before the other as any tension on that pair will destroy the shape of the tally. When pins d and e have been worked, the pair from e along with the pair hanging from f will make the next tally. After working pin g, two rows of ground from top right to lower left can be completed. Pairs hanging from h and i are ready for the tally, and by working ground pins as necessary the diamond can be finished.

Fig. 60a

Raised tally (Figs 61a and 61b) Added variety is introduced by using both cloth and half stitch in the same diamond. Work to pin a. Take the two centre passive pairs and make the tally twice the usual length. Place a thick pin on top of the tally. Place the ends of the threads over the pin (Fig. 60b). Carefully ease the tally over the pin and pull the threads into position. Work half stitch with these pairs. The weaver at a works to b in half stitch. Complete the diamond.

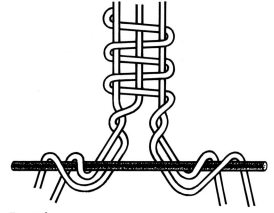

Fig. 60b

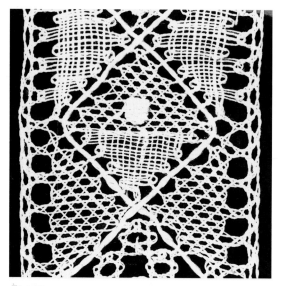

Fig. 61a

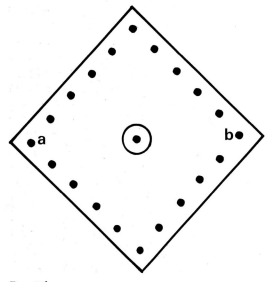

Fig. 61b

Tallies in Torchon ground – an alternative method (Figs 62a and 62b) Work pins a to f inclusive in half stitch, pin, half stitch. Twist all pairs once more as they are to be used for tallies. Make tallies with pairs from a and b, c and d, e and f, being sure to leave the weaver on the left lower side of the finished tally. Work the next diagonal row of ground from pin g from right to left, and this anchors the tallies firmly in position. The next diagonal row is worked normally as the first row, and the following row with the tallies as the second row.

Rose ground (Fig. 63) There are several variations of rose ground. Refer to the pattern on page 21 where cloth stitch and twist was used between each unit. Half stitch only is used in this sampler. Refer back to Fig. 36 on page 23. Stitches without pins, a, b, g and h are worked in half stitch.

Gimp threads: when no longer required they are overlapped as shown in the photograph, laid back over the work and cut off later.

To complete the sampler (Fig. 64) Work half of the cloth stitch diamond. Twist all pairs once. Continue weaving leaving out two pairs each side at the points and one at each of the remaining edge pins. Knot each pair with a reef knot. At one side leave one long thread for sewing and trim the others to 10mm. Place the threads back over the cloth stitch, fold the dia-

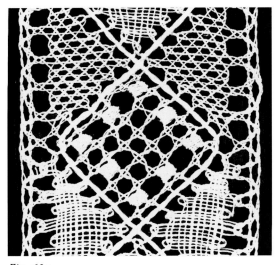

Fig. 62a

Fig. 63

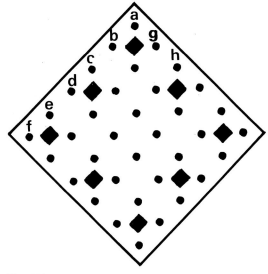

Fig. 62b

mond back to make a straight end. Use the long thread to sew this into position, trapping the ends inside. The diamond at the beginning is treated similarly to make a firm edge.

Note: An alternative method when the point is to be retained is explained on page 45.

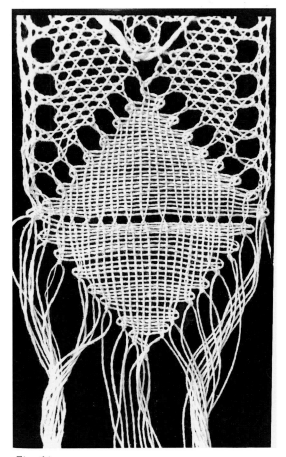

Fig. 64

Fig. 65

A DECORATION WITH HALF STITCH EDGE

Requirements: Twenty-six pairs of bobbins and one gimp pair. Refer to Fig. 65.
Prepare pricking 66.

To begin (Fig. 67) Hang all pairs round the top pin, a. Use the left side two bobbins as weaver and weave half stitch through all pairs to pin b. Continue in half stitch but work cloth stitch and twist either side of the edge pins as described on page 19. Work from c to d through thirteen pairs and put the pin between the last pairs worked. Cover with half stitch, both become weavers and continue on each side. The diagram clarifies the method. Note that the left side gimp thread from cloth diamond e travels round f and when this is com-

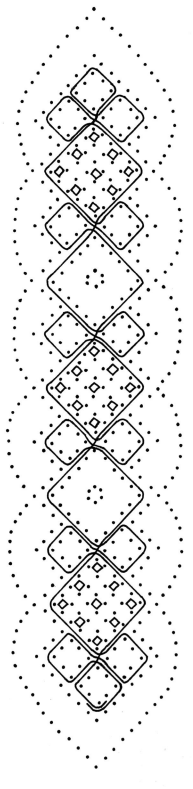

Fig. 66

Fig. 67

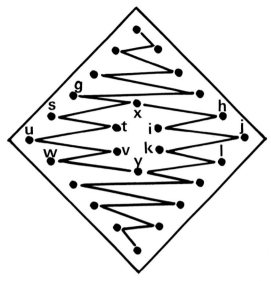

Fig. 68

plete round g. The gimp threads lie together, there are no twists between.

Hole in cloth (Fig. 68) Work the cloth stitch diamond to pin g. Weave back through four pairs, place pin x between and cover. Both pairs become weavers, work h, i, j, k, l and back to the centre. Work s, t, u, v, w and back through the other weaver, put up pin y and cover it. Complete the diamond with the right hand weaver pair.

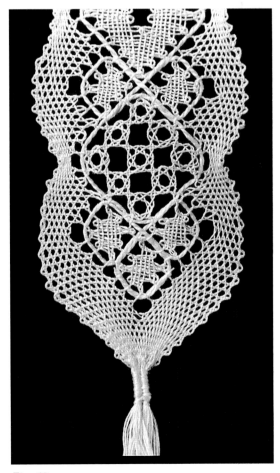

Fig. 69

Fig. 70

To complete lace (Fig. 69) Work in half stitch to the point but do not put in the pin.

Isolate the outside pair on each side and divide the centre pairs into two groups (Fig. 70). Take the left pair over the centre left group, and right pair under the centre right group. Cross the pairs right over left. Take the new left pair under and over the left group and the new right pair over and under the right group. Cross the pairs right over left. Pull the pairs tightly and ease them closely together. Continue for the desired length. The threads are knotted together in pairs. Cut the threads to leave a tassle.

DECORATION A

Requirements: Twenty pairs of bobbins
Refer to Figs 71 and 72. Prepare pricking 73.

To begin Hang three pairs round pin a, two pairs round pin b and one pair on each of the remaining pins. Use the right hand pair from a

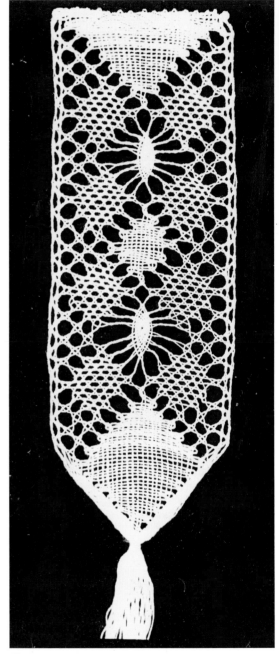

Fig. 71

as weaver and work in cloth stitch to b. Work through the pairs on b, remove the pin and replace it to the right of the pin. Continue to c, leaving out two pairs after a and b and one at the other pins. Pairs from d and e work the footside pins.

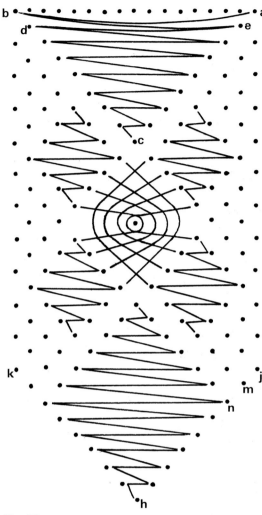

Fig. 72

To complete at a point Complete the lace to the
point h. Two pairs will hang from j, k and h
and one from the other pins. The pair from m
weaves half stitch through the two pairs from j,
leave it on the edge. The pair from n weaves
half stitch through three pairs to the outside
edge. Try to keep these stitches as close to the
cloth diamond as possible. Continue in this
manner until the pair from h works through
nine pairs. Complete the other side in the
same way. Take the outside pairs and cross
them over and under the threads and knot
them firmly to make a tassel. Ease the side half
stitch until it is close and neat. The half stitch
is worked without pins.

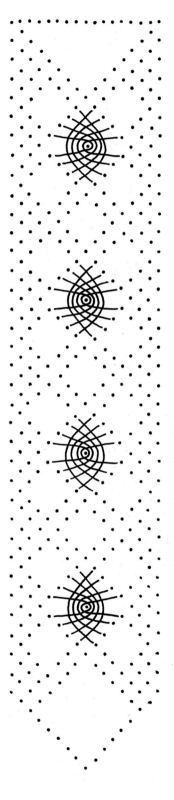

Fig. 73

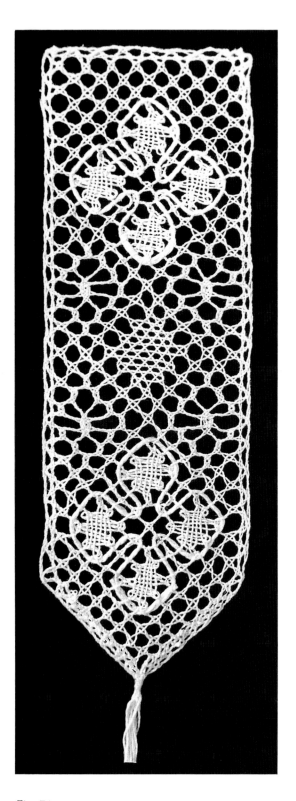

Fig. 74

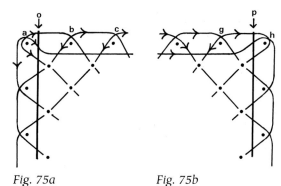

Fig. 75a   *Fig. 75b*

DECORATION B

Requirements: Twenty pairs of bobbins and
one gimp pair. Refer to Figs 74, 75a and
75b. Prepare pricking 76.

To work the top edge (Fig. 75b) Hang four pairs
round pin a, two round pin b and one behind
the pricking at position o. Work cloth stitch
and twist with the threads to the right of pin a.
Take the right pair through the pair from o with
cloth and twist, and place it behind pin b to
fall to the right of the other pairs. The pair to
the right of a and the pair from o work cloth
stitch and twist. This pair becomes the twisted
passive that runs horizontally across the lace.
Work cloth stitch and twist with the threads to
the right of pin b. Hang two pairs round pin c
and allow this pair to fall behind the pin and
to the right of them. The right hand threads
work cloth stitch and twist. Continue until
pairs have been added at g. The passive pair
continues to pass through pairs hanging from
b, c to g with cloth stitch and twist. Add a pair
at position p and use the top passive pair at
corner pin h. The diagram clarifies the method.

The result is better when the outer thread is
twisted twice. To avoid undue complication
this has been omitted and can be used when
the method is fully understood.

Note that cloth stitch and twist, pin, cloth
stitch and twist has been used in the Torchon
ground surrounding the spider.

To complete at a point Work to pin q and complete the footside at r. Take the pair from s through two passive pairs and work footside pin t, return through two pairs. Take the pair from u through three passive pairs and work footside pin v. Discard the centre passive pair and return through the remaining two pairs. Continue discarding the centre passive pair after each footside pin has been worked. Work the other side similarly and at the point tie the threads in a tight bundle. Trim the discarded pairs close to the lace.

Fig. 76

A Cluny collar: see pages 96–100.

3. Bedfordshire or Beds-Maltese Lace

The distinctive features of Bedfordshire lace are the plaits with picots, leaves and trails of cloth stitch which move continuously through the design. The name – Bedfordshire – indicates the type of lace, for it was made throughout the East Midland counties. It is also known as Beds-Maltese lace, but the laces of Malta usually have a Maltese cross worked in cloth stitch. The simple Cluny laces have similar techniques but may be identified by a scallopped headside and plait or leaf pairs which pass straight through trails which usually have twisted pairs.

Explanation of Terms used

To hang pairs on a pin To hang pairs in order on a pin, to cover a pin. Refer to page 11.

The footside This is worked differently from Torchon in that there are more passive pairs – these may be either twisted or straight.

The plait, also known in some districts as the Leg This is made using two pairs in continuous half stitch without pins.

Ninepin This is the name given to a traditional arrangement of plaits and picots on the headside.

The leaf, also known as the plait This is the effect obtained by using two pairs of bobbins, and weaving one thread about the other three.

The trail This is a continuous strip of cloth or half stitch which forms a prominent part of the pattern. It serves to take in or release pairs, plaits or leaves to facilitate the working of the rest of the design.

The crossing of four plaits or leaves, also known as the Windmill This occurs when two plaits meet at a pin. Refer to page 54.

The crossing of six plaits This occurs when three plaits meet at a pin. Refer to page 57.

The crossing of eight plaits This occurs when four plaits meet at a pin. Refer to page 85.

Basic Stitches

The Plait (Fig. 77) Use the four threads, make a half stitch, and repeat half stitches for the required length. It is not usual to count the number of stitches but to estimate by the appearance of the work. In order to achieve a close and flat plait pull the pairs of threads

Fig. 77

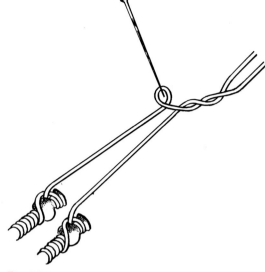

Fig. 78a

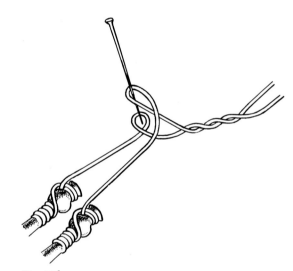

Fig. 78b

well apart between each half stitch to improve the tension and to keep the plait firm.

The Picot This is the decorative loop found on the plait. In fine thread it is always worked with two threads to give it weight and maintain the loop when laundered. If thick thread is used a single-thread picot is adequate.

1   *Set to the left of the plait using fine thread* (Figs 78a and 78b) Take the two left hand threads of the plait, and twist three times. Take a pin in the right hand and hold it – point to the left – over the extreme left thread. Bring the point under the thread towards the worker and over into the picot hole. Keep it loosely around the pin. Take the other thread and put it around the same pin, bringing it to the front and clockwise behind. Twist the two threads together three times more, and pull tightly together. The threads should run twisted together about the pin to form a sound double picot.

If the threads remain as two separate loops when the pin is removed the picot is incorrect. This happens when threads are tightened separately before the final twists are added.

2   *Set to the right of the plait using fine thread* (Figs 79a and 79b) Twist the two right hand threads of the plait three times. Take a pin in the right hand and hold it – point towards the left – under the right hand thread, bring the point over the thread

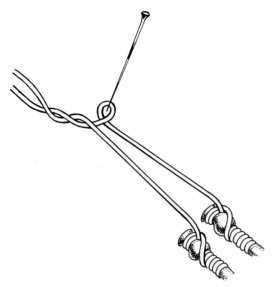

Fig. 79a

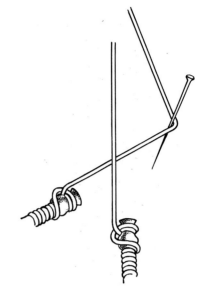

Fig. 80a

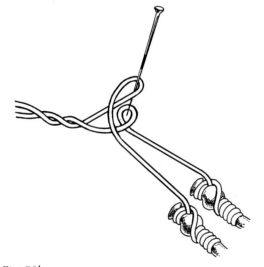

Fig. 79b

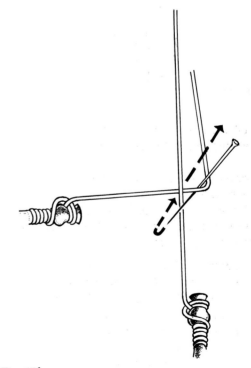

Fig. 80b

towards the worker, and into the picot hole.
Take the other thread and bring it in front
and behind the pin in an anti-clockwise
direction. Twist the pair three times and
pull tightly together.

3 *Set to the left of the plait using thick thread*
   (Figs 80a, 80b and c) Take the two left
   hand threads of the plait in the left hand
   and hold them taut. Take a pin in the right
   hand, put it under the right of these two
   threads, and pull the left thread across

underneath it (a) so that the threads are
crossed. Bring the pin towards the worker
over the crossed threads, then turn the
point of the pin away taking it under the
crossed threads and up between them (b).

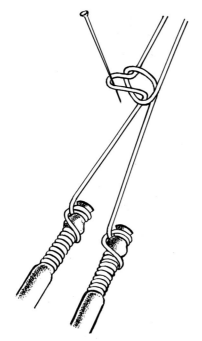

Fig. 80c

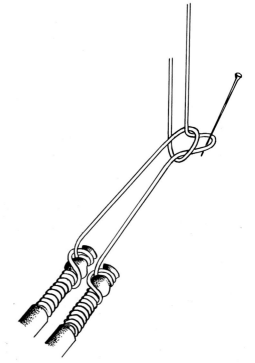

Fig. 80d

Stick the pin into the picot hole to the left of the plait and ease the threads until a single picot thread appears about the pin (c). It is important to manipulate the threads until a single tight picot appears on one side of the plait.

4   Set to the right of the plait using thick thread (Fig. 80d) A very satisfactory picot is achieved if instructions for a picot on the left are followed exactly, and the pin inclined to a hole on the right of the plait.

Note When picots are made on both sides, work one picot and half stitch before making the second picot to avoid a hole in the plait.

Thread To achieve firm plaits and definite picots a linen thread is preferable. The only reliable way of selecting the correct thread is to work a small area of lace, a trail, plait and picots. Each manufacturer has his own system of numbering. The following may be taken as a rough guide for comparing thread thickness.

DMC Broder Machine (cotton)			
30	50	50	—
Madeira Tanne (cotton)			
30	30 or 50	50 or 80	80
Brok (cotton)			
—	80/2	100/3	100/2
Belgian linen: Fresia or Bouc			
80/2	120/2	140/2	140/2

To prepare prickings As far as possible follow instructions on page 3. Prick the nine pin edging and the plait crossings but not the picots to the side of plaits. Separate the photocopy and card, mark in the plaits and leaves. This is easier to understand before the addition of picots. Reassemble the copy and card, hold it up to the light to ensure that this is correct, prick in the picots. Alternatively prick the picots 'by eye'.

Note When working the lace the overall appearance is important. For example, the plaits are usually in a straight line. This will take priority over the number of pinholes in a trail between the plaits, tallies or leaves.

PLAITED LACE NO. 1

Requirements: Eight pairs of bobbins, Madeira Tanne no. 30. Refer to Figs 81 and 82. Prepare pricking 83.

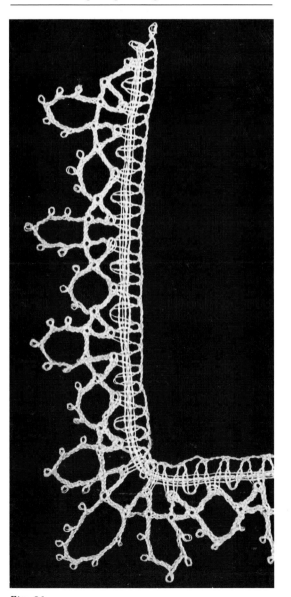

Fig. 81

Fig. 82

Hang two pairs on A1, and two pairs in order on B. Hang two pairs in order on C and two pairs on D.

To begin at the footside Using the two pairs hanging at A1, twist the threads to the right of the pin three times, and work cloth stitch and twist to cover the pin. Give each pair one extra twist. In future that stitch will be referred to as *cloth stitch and two twists*. (Reference may be made to *cloth stitch and twist twice* – this instruction requires that cloth stitch and twist be worked through two pairs). Discard the right-hand pair. Take the inner (left hand) pair, and work cloth stitch through the two pairs hanging at B. Twist the weaver twice and put up pin 2 to the right of the weaver pair.

To work the footside When instructions require that the next footside pin be worked, proceed as follows. Take the fourth pair from the outside edge, and work cloth stitch through two pairs towards the edge. Twist the weaver twice, and with the outside pair work cloth stitch and two twists. Put up the pin inside two pairs (in this case pin 3). Ignore the outer pair and with

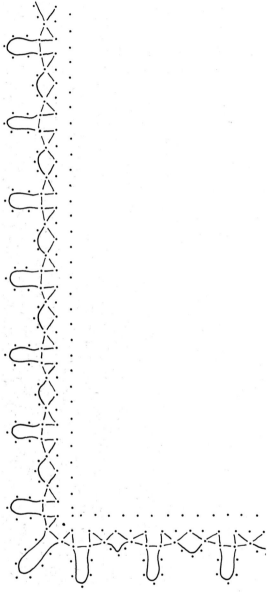

Fig. 83

and ease the pairs down. Work the footside and pin 5.

Put up pin 6 as pin 2, and repeat the footside and pin 7. Remember to complete the sequence and leave the weaver as fourth pair from the outside edge.

The plait Using the two pairs hanging from pin 4, plait as far as pin-hole 8, but do not put up the pin.

The crossing of four plaits The pairs at D are introduced at pin 8. Normally they will be in the lace as a plait. However, it is neat and easy to join in the pairs at a crossing rather than have a short unattached plait at the beginning. Pairs from D and pairs from the plait from pin 4 will make the crossing.

To work a four plait crossing (Fig. 84) Use the two plaits and consider them as four pairs. Use each pair as a single bobbin is used in cloth stitch. Place the second over the third. At the same time place the fourth over the third and the second over the first. Put up the pin (in this case pin 8). Place the second over the third. The plaits have crossed each other.

To continue Follow the black lines which indicate the position of the plaits. Plait from pin 8 the left hand pair work cloth stitch through two pairs to the left.

To join in pairs for a plait Using the same weaver, work in cloth stitch through the two pairs hanging at C. Twist the weaver twice, and put up pin 4 to the right of the weaver. Work cloth stitch back through these two pairs, and then discard them to the left of the pillow for use later. Remove the support pins at C and B

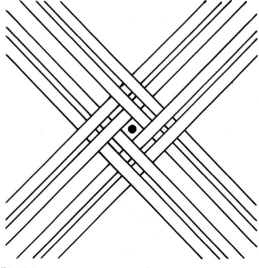

Fig. 84

as far as pin 9. Take the fourth pair from the right (weaver), and work cloth stitch through the two pairs of the plait. Put up pin 9 to the right of the weaver, and work back through the plait pairs. Work the footside and pin 10.

Plait the other two pairs at pin 8 and the pairs hanging from pin 9. Make a crossing at pin 11. Plait the right hand pairs ready for use at 17 and the left hand pairs as far as 12, where a picot is made to the left of the plait. Select the correct picot for the thread being used. Continue plaiting, making picots at 13, 14, 15 and 16. In order to keep the picot at 14 tight to the plait, it is necessary after that pin to keep the threads in a straight line from pin 13, and to turn the plait only when it is the correct length to work the picot at 15. Continue plaiting as far as 17 where a crossing of plaits is made using this plait and the plait from pin 11. Plait in both directions ready for use.

Work the fourth pair from the right (weaver) through the right hand plait from 17 in cloth stitch. Put up pin 18 and work in cloth stitch back through the plait pairs. Plait these pairs and with the plait from 17 make a crossing at 19. Use the left hand pairs to plait to 8, making picots at 20, 21 and 22. Take the right hand pairs and plait to 4. Work the footside pin 1.

It is now possible to put up pin 2 and follow the instructions through again.

The corner Follow the markings on the pricking which indicate the plaits. The footside is worked normally to V – the same position as 18 – and the normal footside sequence is worked with the corner pin X. Pin Y is put up and the footside repeated using pin X for the second time. The weaver works through the plait which has made the corner ninepin, and pin Z – the same position as 9 – is put up.

PLAITED LACE NO. 2

Requirements: Ten pairs of bobbins,
Madeira Tanne no. 30.
Refer to Figs 85 and 86.
Prepare pricking 87.

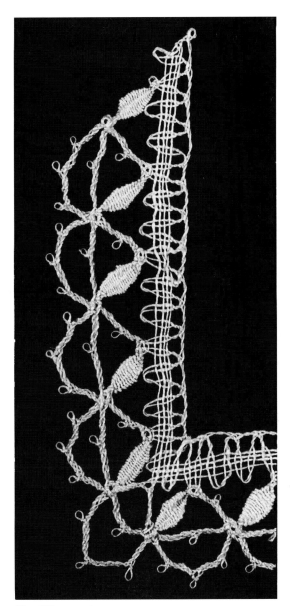

Fig. 85

Hang two pairs on each of pins A1, C, D and E, and two pairs in order on B. Work exactly as for the previous pattern as far as pin 5 with the footside completed and the weaver in position as fourth pair from the outside edge.

To make a leaf (Fig. 88) This fills the space between 4 and 6 and is made using the pairs left out after pin 4. Take the two pairs, and work a cloth stitch being careful to pull it up

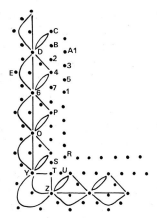

Fig. 86

very closely. Lengthen the thread which completed the stitch. Take it to the right under the
outside thread, and back over it. Take it under
the centre thread, over the left hand thread,
back under it, and over the centre thread.
Weaving in this manner is continued for the
length required.

In order to achieve a neat edge to the leaf,
the weaving thread must be kept evenly about
the outside threads, which determine the
shape of the leaf. The outside threads are held
one in either hand, the right hand thread bobbin being kept between the third and fourth
fingers so that the weaver bobbin can be held
between the thumb and forefinger. The weaver
should be manipulated until the thread fits
snugly about the outside threads, which must
be kept widely apart to assist in the shaping of
the leaf. In the beginning it is necessary to pull
the weaver thread fairly closely to achieve a
pointed effect. At least three quarters of the
leaf is worked before any adjustment is made
to bring it to a point. The weaver thread is
gradually tightened to obtain the correct effect.
The leaf is completed with cloth stitch.

This is probably one of the most difficult
techniques to manage well. Practice is necessary to perfect the shape.

To continue the pattern The pairs hanging at E
would normally make a plait with picots on the
headside, and the pairs hanging at D would
also be plaited. However these pairs are
brought directly into the pattern at the crossing

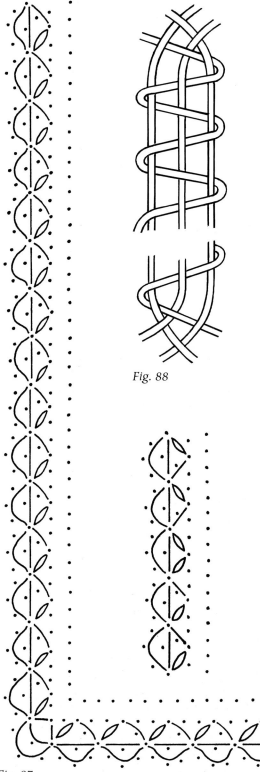

Fig. 88

Fig. 87

at 6 as it is the beginning of the lace. Also to come in at pin 6 is the leaf from pin 4.

Six plait crossing (Fig. 89) Six pairs from three plaits hang ready for use. Treat each pair as a single thread, keeping them together throughout the working. Spread the pairs well out on the pillow for easy identification.

   Take the right centre pair over the next pair to the right. Take the left centre pair under the next pair to the left. Cross the new centre pairs right over left. Put up the pin between them. Take the pair to the right of the pin out to the right over the next pair and under the outside pair. Take the pair to the left of the pin out to the left under the next pair and over the outside pair.

   Find the new centre pairs, and take the right pair over the next pair to the right. Take the left centre pair under the next pair to the left. Cross the new centre pairs right over left. Take the right centre pair over the next pair to the right. Take the left centre pair under the next pair to the left. Remove support pins D and E. Pull up into position. The pairs are ready for use as plaits or leaves.

To continue the pattern Plait the left hand pairs with picots to O. Plait the centre pairs with picot to O. Plait the right hand pairs with picot to P. Return to the footside and the weaver which should be fourth pair from the outside edge, put up pin 7, and work the complete footside sequence including pin 1. The pattern is complete.

The corner A clear neat corner is achieved by changing the passive pairs on the footside. Study the photograph as the lace is worked.

   Work the footside normally and put up pin S, weave back through two passive pairs, and leave the weaver hanging to become the new right hand passive pair after the corner. Plait the two right hand pairs from the crossing at Y to the corner at T, and put up pin T between them. Weave the right hand pair through the two passive pairs, and leave it hanging to become the new left passive pair after the corner. Take the old left hand passive pair, which

is now lying to the right of pin T, and the remaining half of the plait, and plait them together to Z. Put pin U to the right of the old remaining right hand passive pair.

   Turn the pillow. Take this pair which lies to the left of pin U and work the footside sequence using pin R for a second time. Note that the weaver passes through the two new passive pairs which fall from S and T.

Pattern reversal This is necessary to achieve a symmetrical corner. A leaf is worked out from the footside to the corner at Y, and to correspond, a leaf is worked from Z into the footside. After the corner has been turned, all leaves are worked into the footside and plaits worked out from it. At a centre point the leaf worked into the footside is worked out again as another leaf.

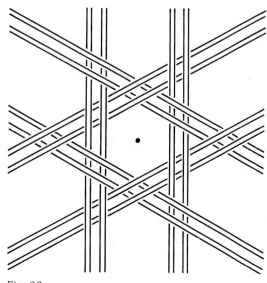

Fig. 89

PLAITED LACE NO. 3 OVAL MAT EDGING

> *Requirements:* Twelve pairs of bobbins,
> Madeira Tanne 30. Refer to Fig. 90.
> Prepare pricking 91 × 130%.

The footside (Figs 92 and 93) Hang two pairs
round pin A1, twist the right threads three
times and cover the pin with cloth stitch and
two twists. Work through two passive pairs and
work the footside to c: remember to introduce
two pairs at b.

Fig. 91

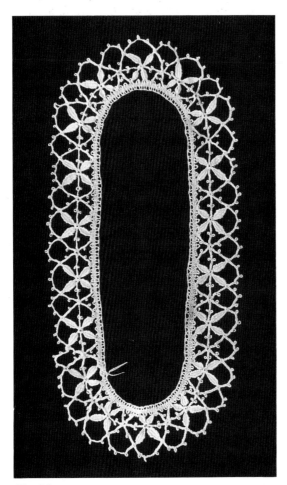

Fig. 90

Plaits and leaves Plait from b to d. Hang two
pairs round each of pins C and D. At d work a
six plait crossing with these and the plait pairs.
Remove pins C and D. Plait to c, f and e with
picots as necessary. Link in the plait pairs at c
and work the footside to g. Hang two pairs
round a support pin behind e and use these
and the plait pairs for a four plait crossing at e.
Make leaves from e and c and using the plait
from d, make a six plait crossing at f. Continue.

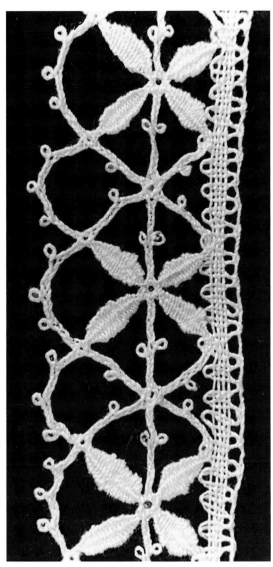

Fig. 92

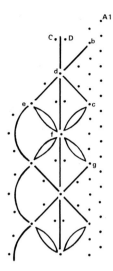

Fig. 93

Fig. 94

CIRCULAR EDGING

Requirements: as above. Refer to Fig. 94.
Prepare pricking 95.

This is worked in the same way as the previous
pattern.

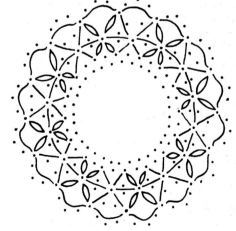

Fig. 95

BOOKMARK

Requirements: Ten pairs of bobbins,
Madeira Tanne 30. Refer to Figs 96 and
97. Prepare pricking 98.

Hang two pairs round pin A, twist threads
each side of the pin three times and work cloth
stitch to cover the pin. With the same threads
make one half stitch. Place four pairs vertically
so that four bobbins hang back over the end of
the pillow. Put pins between the thread and
neck of the bobbin to prevent the bobbins
moving forward. Use the four hanging threads
as two pairs and work a four plait crossing at b
with the pairs from A. Plait with the left side
pairs making picots at c, d and e.

Turn the pillow and remove the four pins
holding the bobbins at the back of the pillow
in position. Plait to K, making picots at g, h
and j. Hang two pairs round K and work K as
A. Work a four plait crossing at 1 and continue
to m. Work the leaves to the centre, hang two
pairs at position x and work a six plait crossing
at q. Remove pin x. On the right, plait with
picots to p. It is preferable to leave the picots
until the leaves have been made as this allows
more space for manoeuvre. Continue.

To complete the lace Make the six plait crossing
at r. The centre plait can be made to w but the
following alternative is given to explain how
threads may be disposed of safely and almost
invisibly.

At r take six threads for the leaf. Use two as
one on the inner threads and work the cloth
stitch. The double threads are now on the outside and will remain so while the leaf is
worked. Retain the double threads and work
the plait crossing at s. Discard the extra
threads by putting them back over the work.
Knots are unnecessary and later the threads
will be cut off. Work half stitch and the picot at
t. The four pairs now work as single threads to
plait to u. Discard the two inner threads and
use the outer two to make picot u. Continue
with two singles and two doubles. Discard the
other extra threads before w. Work the other
side similarly. Make a crossing at w and plait

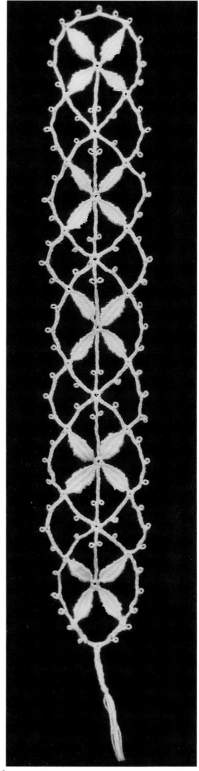

Fig. 96

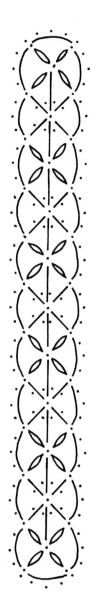

Fig. 98

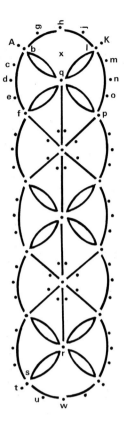

Fig. 97

HALF STITCH CIRCLE AND TRAIL PATTERN

Requirements: Seventeen pairs of bobbins and two extra pairs for the corner, DMC Broder Machine no. 30. Refer to Figs 99 and 100. Prepare pricking 101.

Hang two pairs round A1, two pairs in order on B, four in order on D and one on C. Begin the footside as in previous patterns and work to pin 2, twist the weaver twice and put up the pin. The pair on C is trail weaver, work to the right with cloth stitch through the pairs from D, twist the weaver twice and put up pin d. The weaver is always twisted twice at the end of the row. Work a kiss between weavers from d and 2:

Crossing weavers, often known as a 'kiss' The weavers work cloth stitch and two twists.

using double threads. To finish the plait, knot threads one and three, two and four, three and five and so on. Take the outside threads under and over all the threads and tie tightly. Use reef knots throughout.

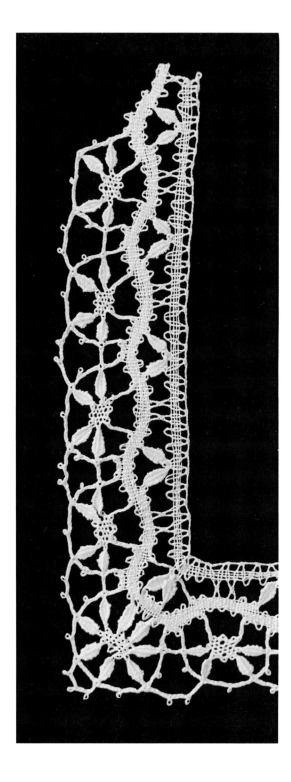

Fig. 100

Having changed position, each continues to work the other's trail. Work the trail through the four passive pairs to e, continue to f and g. Join in two pairs for a leaf at h. Similarly add two pairs at j but include them in the trail and leave them out after pin k. Make a leaf from h and link it into the footside at 8. Continue the footside to the next 'kiss'. Make the leaf and continue the trail to include the leaf pairs at n. Work back through six pairs to o. Remember to return to the left side of the trail through four pairs – two pairs are left out after o for the plait to complete the circle. Continue to p.

Fig. 99

the weaver one twist more and put up pin t. Weave back including the leaf pairs from r. Twist the weaver once more and put up pin u. Continue weaving in half stitch but work cloth stitch and twist either side of pins v and w. Work to x and back to y. Weave back through three pairs only, put up pin z to the left of the weaver and cover with cloth stitch in preparation for the next leaf. Make leaves from y and z. Continue the plait from r, work the crossings and plait to j. Plait from x to the trail, work the 'kisses' as indicated and continue.

The corner Join in two extra pairs at c. Make the leaf to o, continue, following the diagram and take the pairs back into the circle at e. Complete the circle. The extra threads can be removed in the leaves as described in the previous pattern.

The footside Pin X is used twice. When the weaver has linked in the plait at Y and released it for the leaf, it remains in that position waiting for the leaf to return. Then pin Y is removed and used a second time to link in the leaf and release it for a plait.

HANDKERCHIEF CORNER

Requirements: Seventeen pairs of bobbins for the edging and pairs as required for the plaits and leaves (twenty pairs). Refer to Fig. 102. Prepare pricking 103.

At pin a on the pricking add two pairs for a leaf. Pairs for leaves or plaits are added on the trail. These work across the pillow – with crossings as necessary – to the diagonal footside line.

The Cluny method of linking plaits into a trail (Fig. 104) This is very suitable as it ensures a firm result. Use the weaver to work through both plait pairs as usual. Put up the pin between the plait pairs (i.e. to the right of two pairs) and cover the pin with cloth stitch. The weaver from the footside has become part of the plait and the left hand pair from the plait has become the weaver. This method ensures good tension.

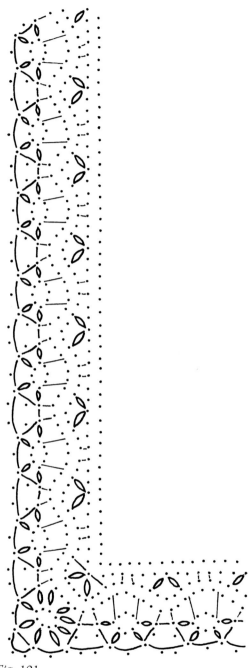

Fig. 101

Hang two pairs round each of E and F and plait from k introducing the new pairs at four plait crossings at q and r. Make a plait from o and leaves from r and q. Place pin s between the leaf pairs from q and cover with half stitch. Work half stitch through the plait from o, give

After the corner turn the pillow. The plait and leaf pairs become part of the trail and are discarded. Work as follows: the weaver is on the left side of the trail and about to work across to include the plait pairs – lay two alternate threads back from the trail and weave across through the remaining trail pairs and the new plait pairs. Put up the pin to support the weaver and work back across the trail. Then lay back two more alternate threads and continue. It is important that the plait pairs are not discarded until they have travelled securely within the trail. Refer to page 00 for completion and mounting.

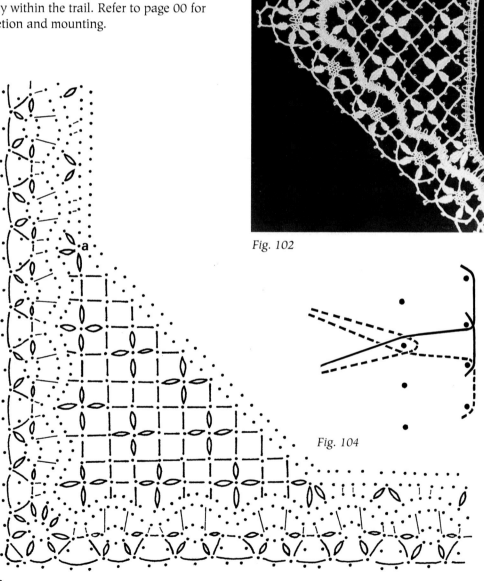

Fig. 102

Fig. 104

Fig. 103

CIRCULAR EDGING

Requirements: Eighteen pairs of bobbins, Madeira Tanne no. 30. Refer to Figs 105 and 106. Prepare two prickings from Fig. 107. Each is a quarter of the circle, use them alternately. The feature in the trail is achieved by twisting the weaver once or twice between the centre passive pairs. To avoid confusion this will not be mentioned below.

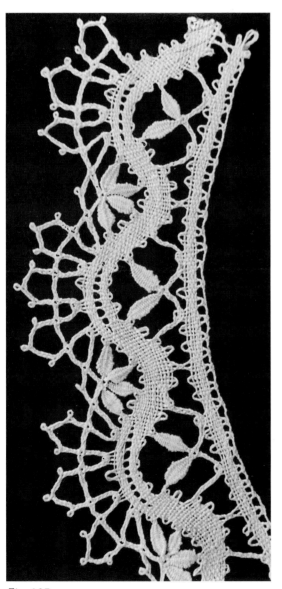

Fig. 105

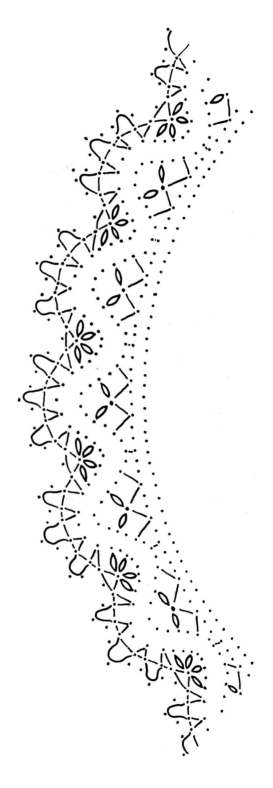

Fig. 107

Hang two pairs round A1, twist the pairs to the right of the pin three times and cover with cloth stitch and two twists. Weave the left side pair through three passive pairs from support pin B. Put up pin 2 and twist the weaver twice. Hang a trail weaver on C and weave through eight pairs from support pin D. Twist the weaver twice and put up pin d. Cross the weavers with cloth stitch and two twists and continue the trail. Pairs from the trail are left out for plait at e and leaf at f. Pairs are joined in for the plait at g. Plait from g to h and work a four plait crossing with two pairs from support pin E. Remove pins D and E. Continue the ninepin and trail to j. Ease the pairs from e and f into position and make plait and leaf. Continue the footside, linking in the plait at k, work to m. Plait from k to n and make a four plait crossing. Make the leaf to o and plait to m. The trail weaver at j weaves, bringing in the leaf pairs at o and leaving out pairs for leaves at p and q. Leaves and plait work a six plait crossing at r and leaves are made back to the trail at s and t. Continue.

CROSSING TRAILS AND LEAF PATTERN

Requirements: Twenty-two pairs of bobbins, DMC Broder Machine no. 30. Refer to Figs 108 and 109. Prepare pricking 110. Picots may be added if required, refer to the photograph.

In this pattern the method for crossing trails is practised, and a different arrangement of passive threads in the footside is introduced. In Bedfordshire lace the footside is worked at the discretion of the worker, but thought must be given to achieve a balance of cloth, half stitch, plaits and leaves.

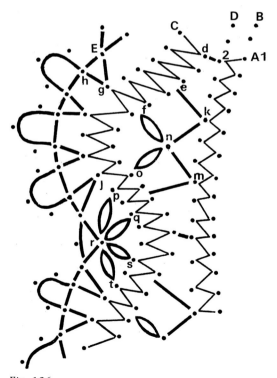

Fig. 106

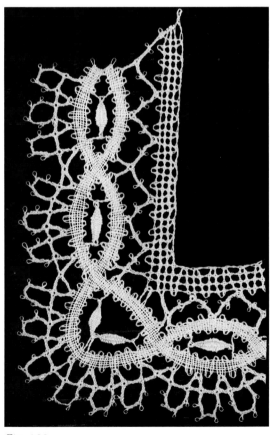

Fig. 108

Hang two pairs on A1, three pairs in order on B, two pairs in order on C and two pairs on D. Hang one pair on E and three pairs in order on F from right to left. Hang four pairs in order on G from left to right, and one pair on H. Hang two pairs in order on I, and two pairs on J.

To work the footside with twisted pairs Twist the right hand pair three times, and cover pin A1 with cloth stitch and twist. Give the right hand pair an extra twist, and discard to the right. Take the other pair as weaver, and work cloth stitch and twist through the next three pairs hanging from B. These pairs will remain as twisted passive pairs. Weave through the two pairs hanging from C in cloth stitch. Twist the weaver twice and put up pin 2. Weave back to the right in cloth stitch through the two pairs, which are then left out for a plait. Continue weaving through four pairs to the right in cloth stitch and twist. Put up pin 3 inside two pairs, twist the outer pair once more, and discard to the right. Take the inner pair back through three passive pairs in cloth stitch and twist. Twist the weaver twice and put up pin 4. Continue the footside using this arrangement of pairs. Remove pins at B and C.

Plaits Plait with picots the pairs from 2, remembering to make a half stitch in the plait between the picots. Using these pairs and pairs from D, make a four plait crossing, and then remove the pin at D. Make plaits, and work the footside to link in the plait on that side.

The trails Using the pair at E as weaver, work cloth stitch to the left through the three pairs hanging at F. Using the pair at H as weaver, work cloth stitch to the right through four pairs hanging at G. The weavers are side by side; cloth stitch them together, put up pin a, and cover with another stitch. These pairs work out, one each way, as weavers for the cloth trails.

   On the right side weave through the three trail pairs, and on through one more pair, i.e. half the plait. Put up pin b and weave back through four pairs, and put up pin c. Take care not to take in the weaver for the left hand side. Continue with this trail and bring in the other half of the plait at pin d. After pin e leave out the edge passive pair which will become part of the leaf.

   On the left side take the weaver hanging from pin a, cloth stitch through the four pairs, and put up a pin at j. Continue weaving but before putting up pin 1 work through the two pairs hanging from I leaving these out after the pin for the ninepin edge plait. After pin m leave out the edge passive pair to become the other half of the leaf. Remove support pins F, G and I.

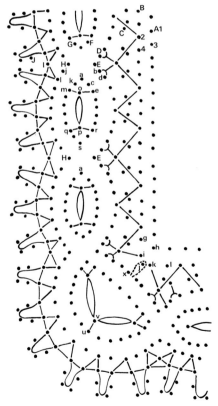

Fig. 109

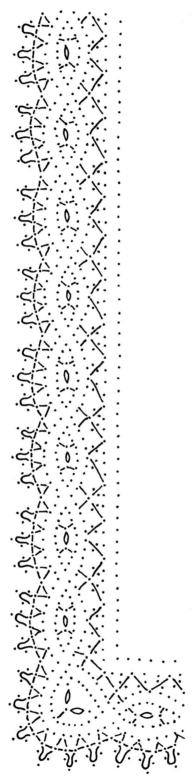

The ninepin Plait the pairs hanging from l and make a four plait crossing with the pairs hanging from J. Remove pin J.

The leaf Using pairs from m and e, twist each pair twice, and work together in half stitch. Put up pin o, and cover with cloth stitch to begin the leaf. Complete the leaf to pin p, and cover with a half stitch. Twist pairs once more.

The crossing of trails Continue each trail, linking in the plaits where necessary, and weaving in the pairs from the leaf at q and r. Cloth stitch the weavers together, and put up pin s. Cover the pin with cloth stitch, weave each back to pinholes H and E, and put up the pins. There are four passive trail pairs on the left, to the right of pin H, and three passive trail pairs on the right, to the left of pin E. When the crossing is completed the same arrangement of pairs must exist for the next pattern repeat. Therefore three pairs from the left side must be transferred to the right side, and all three right hand pairs must go to the left. The left hand pair next to pin H remains unused in that position, and is ignored during the crossing. The three pairs on the left are passed through the three pairs on the right in exactly the same way that the first half of the Torchon spider is worked. This is as follows:

Spread out the six pairs so that they can be easily counted. Take the third pair, and in cloth stitch work towards the right through the remaining three pairs. Still working towards the right, take the second pair through three pairs, and finally the first pair through three pairs. The work must lie flat – the three pairs have passed through in order. One pattern is now complete.

Fig. 110

To continue the pattern to the corner, take the weaver to the left of pin H, and work through four pairs – one pair that remained on that side and three that have crossed over. On the other side, the weaver to the right of pin E works to the left through three pairs that have crossed over. Cloth stitch the weavers together, and put up pin a and cover.

The corner Trails can be seen in the photograph, and the working is straightforward. At u, the weaver is twisted five times, then worked through the leaf pairs, and a pin put up at v. The weaver works back through the leaf pairs, it is twisted five times, and worked back across the trail.

left of the three passive pairs after the corner has been turned. Work it through the next two pairs to the right. The three new passive pairs are now complete, one hanging from j and two from i. Before turning the pillow take the two remaining passive pairs on this side and put up pin k between them. Plait ready for use after the corner has been turned.

Turn the pillow. Take the second pair from the right which is the footside weaver at h and work through these three pairs to the left in cloth stitch and twist. Put up pin l and continue.

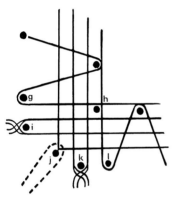

Fig. 111

The footside (Fig. 111) Each pair is indicated by a single line. Cloth stitch and twist is used throughout. The lettering is the same as in Fig. 109.

Work as far as pin h, and put the pin as usual inside two pairs. Leave the threads in this position – do not cover the pin. Plait to pin i and put up the pin in the centre of the plait. Take the right hand pair of the plait and work through the next three pairs of the footside. Take the left hand pair of the plait, and work through the same three passive pairs. The weaver from the inner trail at x is twisted three times and works through the next pair to the right (i.e. the left hand passive pair). Pin j is put up, covered and the weaver returns to the trail. The pair hanging at pin j remains to the

FOUR LEAVES PATTERN

Requirements: Twenty-two pairs of bobbins and two extra pairs for the corner, DMC Broder Machine no. 50. Refer to Figs 112 and 113. Prepare pricking 114. Prick picots as required on plaited ground.

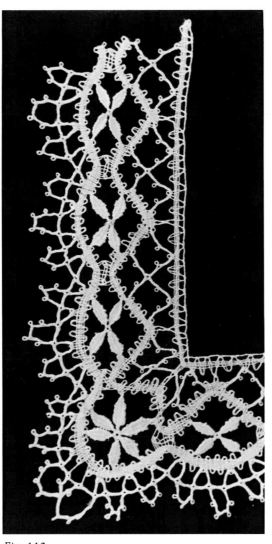

Fig. 112

Hang two pairs round pin A1, two pairs on B and two pairs round C. Begin the footside at A using two passive pairs from pin B. At pin 4 work through the pairs from pin C, these are left out for the plait. Continue the footside to pin 9. One pair on D is trail weaver and works through five pairs from pin E to pin e and back through three pairs to f. Continue the trail to centre pin h. One pair on pin F weaves through five pairs from pin G to pin g and back to pin h. The weavers work cloth stitch, pin h, cloth stitch. The left hand pair temporarily becomes a passive and the right hand pair weaves through three pairs to pin j. Put up the pin and the same weaver travels through nine pairs to pin k. It travels back to the centre through the five left side trail pairs and the other weaver. Put up pin m between them and cover with cloth stitch. Each weaver continues its own trail; there are three pairs in the right side trail and five pairs in the left. Make plaits and a crossing at z. From o to p the weaver passes through five pairs as the pairs from the plait are included. It returns through three as pairs have been left out for the leaf. Again from q it passes through five pairs to r and back to s. A weaver crossing is made at t and the weaver returns through four pairs and loses its weaver function. The next pair to the right become weaver and weaves to the right through the remaining three pairs to u. This weaver returns through the five trail pairs to pin v.

From centre pin m, the left hand weaver works back through five trail pairs and the trail is continued to w where two pairs more are added for the plait. The weaver returns through seven pairs to x and back through five to y. From y the trail contains three pairs only. Plait from w and introduce two pairs at the crossing to work the ninepin headside. Leaves from o and x work the centre crossing.

The corner Pin a is used twice. The inner passive at b and the weaver from the trail at c make a 'kiss' or weaver crossing. In the trail join in two pairs for leaf u. Leaves u, s and t work a six plait crossing, these pairs work leaves x, y and z and are taken into the trails. Discard two pairs in the headside trail.

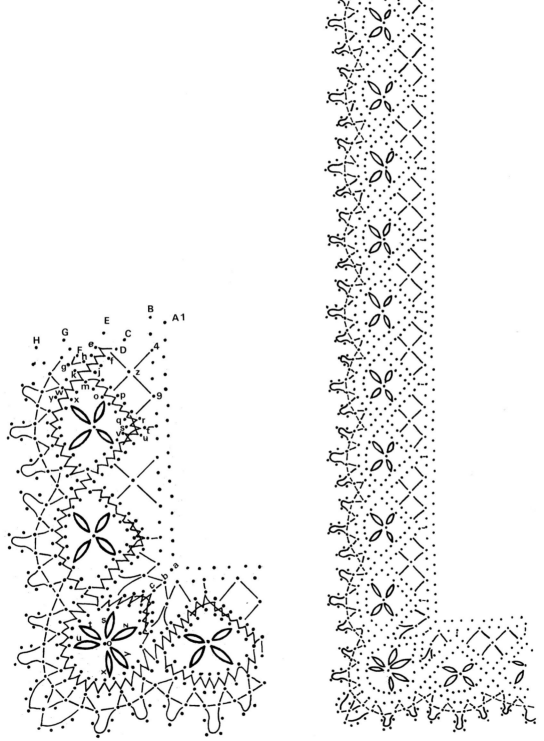

Fig. 113

Fig. 114

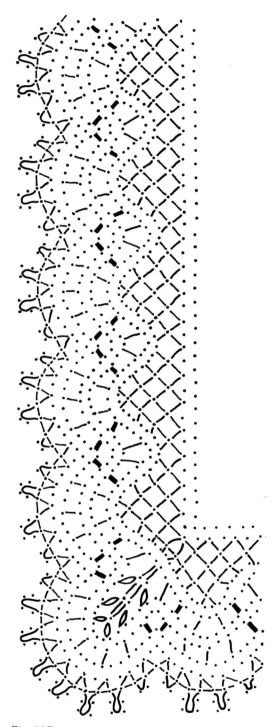

THREE TRAIL PATTERN

Requirements: Thirty-three pairs of bobbins, DMC Broder Machine no. 30. Refer to Figs 115 and 116. Prepare pricking 117.

Fig. 117   *Fig. 115*

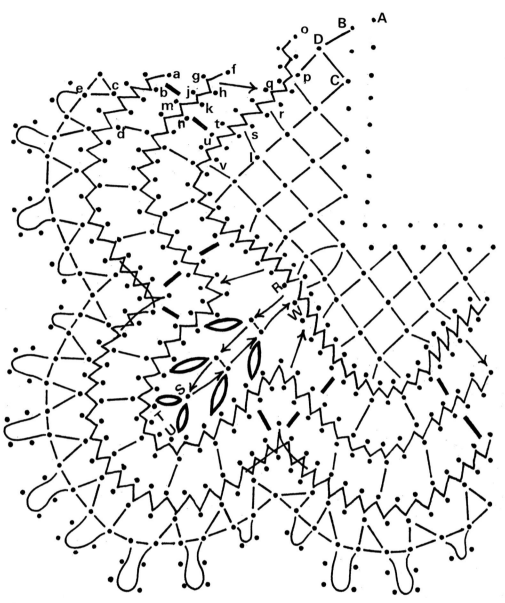

Fig. 116

The footside Hang two pairs round A, twist the right pair three times and cover A with cloth stitch and two twists. Weave across through two passive pairs and two plait pairs from a support pin behind the work. Put up pin B and continue the footside to C. Plait from B to D and introduce two pairs at a four plait crossing. Plait to p.

Left side trail Hang a weaver on a and introduce six pairs into the trail. Leave out one pair after a and b and, introducing two plait pairs at c work the trail to d. Work the ninepin headside introducing the two plait pairs at e.

The centre trail Hang the weaver on f and introduce six pairs into the trail. From g work back through four pairs to h as plait pairs are left out from f. Pairs from a and b make a square leaf or tally, refer to page 39. These pairs are included in the centre trail at j and m. At the same time pairs are left out after k and n for the tally on to the lower trail.

The right side trail Hang a weaver on o and work through six pairs for the inner trail. Link in pairs at p and immediately release them for another plait. Follow the diagram carefully, bring in the plait pairs at q and the tally pairs at t and u. At the same time leave out pairs for plaits at r, s and v.

Contact between trails Use the photograph to check the link. Plaits – marked with arrows on the diagram – are used at the base of the cen-tre trail on the edging and in the corner. The thicker line indicates tallies with pairs left out, but the thin line indicates tallies using trail weavers.

The corner The plait left out at R travels with plait crossings to S. Pin S is placed between the plait pairs which are twisted three times each. The leaf is made and taken into the trail at T and pairs for the next leaf are left out at U. The leaf is made to S and a hook through the hole pulls one of the leaf pairs through. The other leaf threads pass through the loop and the plait is made back to the right side trail at W.

CLOTH STITCH HEADSIDE PATTERN

Requirements: Approximately thirty-two pairs of bobbins, DMC Broder Machine no. 30. Refer to Figs 118 and 119. Prepare pricking 120.

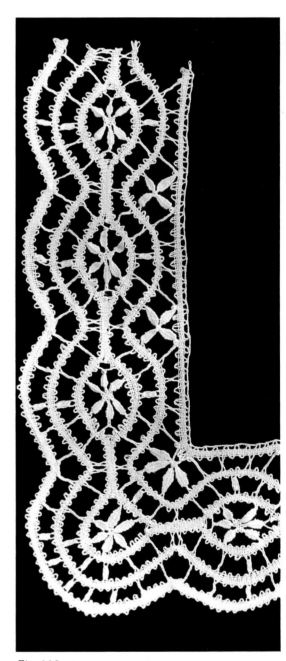

Fig. 118

The number of pairs in each trail is discretionary, according to the wishes of the lacemaker. The tallies at the centre of the head should be worked to maintain a pleasing appearance, rather than counting the number of holes on each repeat.

The footside Hang two pairs round A and work through three passive pairs. Two pairs are added at b for the plait.

The trails The weaver at C works through three passive pairs to d. The weaver from E works through five passive pairs to f. The weaver from G works through three passive pairs to h.

The outer edge The weaver from J works through eight passive pairs to k and the trail is worked to o leaving out pairs at m and n for plaits.

To continue The weavers at h and f cross with cloth stitch and twists. The weaver from f works back for another exchange with the weaver at d: the trails are linked similarly below h and f. Continue to q. Refer to Fig. 121. Place pin p between the plait pairs from m. One pair from the plait from m passes directly through the trail and the other pair becomes the new weaver, thus avoiding any difference in the number of pairs in the trail. Place pin q between the old weaver and pair from the plait.

The weaver from r works through four pairs, put pin s to the right of the weaver and cover it. Both pairs become weavers with two pairs in each trail. Plaits enter trails to increase the passives. Pairs are left out on either side for the centre leaf. The pairs for the other leaves come from the outer plaits. Refer to Fig. 121. Centrally the trails are linked with tallies made using trail weavers.

The corner Leaf t and the corner plait make a four plait crossing at u. The left hand pairs make leaf v and are taken into the trail normally. Pairs are left out for plait w and for leaf x. They are in the wrong position to pass directly through the trail. When the six plait

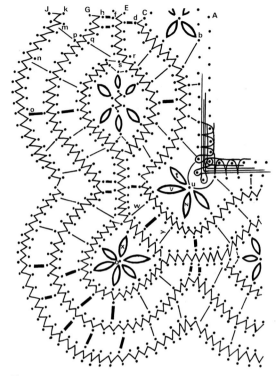

Fig. 119

crossing o has been completed the pillow is turned and the corner completed. Pairs are left out for plait y and leaf z. Make the leaf, remove pin u, use the pairs hanging at the pin and the leaf pairs to make a crossing. Replace the pin and continue.

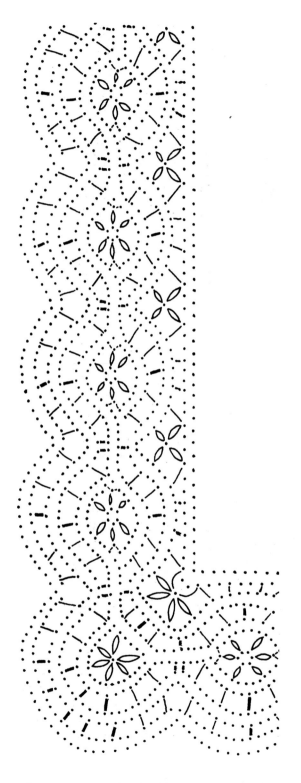

Fig. 120

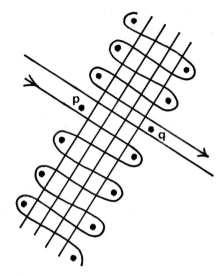

Fig. 121

DIAMOND AND DAISY PATTERN

Requirements: Eighteen pairs of bobbins, Madeira Tanne no. 30, two pairs extra will be required for the corner. Refer to Fig. 122. Prepare pricking 123.

Kat stitch foot (Fig. 124) Before attempting the pattern it is advisable to take four pairs of bobbins and practise this footside. The two lines of holes on the pricking for the Diamond and Daisy pattern may be used.

Put two pairs of bobbins on each of pins P and Q. Twist the outer threads, and work cloth stitch and twist to cover each pin. In some way mark the outer pairs – four rubber bands, one twisted around the shank of each bobbin will identify them temporarily. These are the passive pairs and remain straight throughout. The inner two pairs are the weavers and they are worked together in cloth stitch and twist at R, no pin is put in, and the weavers only cross through each other.

The left hand weaver works through the next pair to the left, pin T is put up, the weaver is twisted once more, and the pin is covered with cloth and twist. The right hand weaver works to the right through the passive pair to the right of it, pin S is put up, the weaver is given one extra twist and the pin covered with cloth

Fig. 122

and twist. The weavers now hang side by side in the middle again, ready to repeat the sequence of stitches and pins. This will begin with the cloth stitch and twist at R, which crosses the weavers without a pin.

When this arrangement is used in the pattern, the right hand side outside edge is worked as described above, but the left hand side is joined into the lace. The join is made by taking the weaver immediately after it has worked through the passive pair, and continuing on through any pairs to be linked in. The pin is put up, the weaver brought back through the pairs joined in, and then through the passive pair to the normal position for crossing the weavers. There is not necessarily a link at every pin.

To work the pattern (Fig. 125a) Hang two pairs on A, and two pairs in order on B to I inclusive.

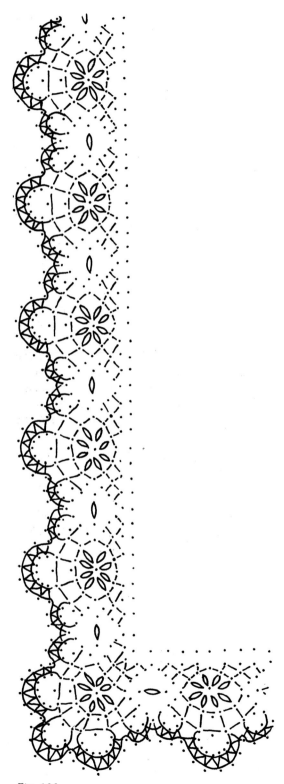

Fig. 123

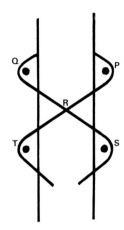

Fig. 124

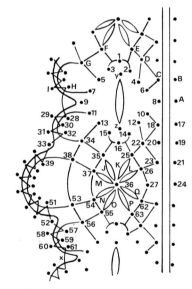

Fig. 125a

The half stitch diamond and raised leaf It is
usual to work the leaf underneath the half
stitch so that the wrong side of the lace is fac-
ing the worker. Take the left hand pair from E
and the right hand pair from F, and make a
half stitch. Put up pin 1 and cover with a half
stitch. The right hand pair becomes the
weaver. Remember that in reality only one
thread travels across the work, but the pair is
known as the weaver pair and the pin at the
end of a row will still go inside two threads.
Weave in half stitch through one pair to the
right (the other pair from E), and put up pin 2.
Weave back to the left, bringing in the other

pair from F, and put up pin 3. Hold the weaver firmly, and remove support pins E and F.

Continue weaving, and bring in both pairs from D at pin 4, and both pairs from G at pin 5. Find the two centre pairs in the half stitch diamond, put up pin y between them, cover with a cloth stitch, and make a leaf as far as z. Place a cloth across these threads and bobbins and ignore them. The cloth will enable the worker to work over them fairly easily .

Take the pair either side of the pin at y, and work one half stitch. This keeps the half stitch close and neat under the leaf. Find the weaver at pin 5, and continue to weave bringing in two pairs from C at 6, H at 7, B at 8, and I at 9. Continue, leaving out two pairs after pins 8, 9, 10 and 11. At pin 12 stop weaving in order to put the leaf threads back into position in the centre of the half stitch.

From pin 12 weave to the left through three pairs of half stitch, through the two leaf pairs, and through four pairs of half stitch. Put up pin 13, and complete the diamond, leaving out two pairs after pins 12 and 13, and one pair after pins 14 and 15. There are two pairs at pin 16 which must be covered with half stitch. As pattern repeats are worked, only one pair enters and leaves at pins 8 and 9, but at the beginning of a strip of lace it is convenient to join in pairs in this manner.

The footside Work the two pairs at pin A, and the two pairs hanging from pin 8 in cloth stitch and twist. Of these four pairs, the middle pairs are weavers and the outside pairs are the passive pairs. The weavers cross in cloth stitch and twist (equivalent to R on the practice strip). The right hand pairs work pin 17, and the left hand weaver passes through the passive pair and through the plait from pin 10. Put up pin 18, and take the weaver back to the right through the plait pairs and through the passive pair. Work pins 19, 20 and 21. Pairs are plaited from 18 and 12, and a crossing made at 22. Work pin 23.

Plaits Plaits from pins 10 and 12 have already been used. Plait the pairs from 14/16 and 15/16 together, also the pairs from 13. Work

four plait crossings at 25 and 26, and plait the right hand pairs from 26 to be linked in with the footside weaver at 27.

The heading Two pairs hanging from pin 9 become weaver and outside passive pair for the scallop, and retain these functions throughout the pattern. The passive pair is twisted and forms the edge curve. It enters and leaves the point of the diamond at pin 9. The weaver does not enter the diamond.

The scallop This is worked as follows: *Use the outside left hand pair as weaver, and work to the right, through the passive in cloth stitch and twist, through the next two pairs in cloth stitch, put up pin 28, and twist the weaver twice. Work to the left through two pairs in cloth stitch, twist the weaver once, and work cloth stitch and twist with the outside pair. Put up pin 29, and twist the weaver once more**.

Work from * to ** pins 30 and 31. Work from * to ** pins 32 and 33. Plait the four threads hanging from the cloth at pin 32 and make a crossing at 34 with the plait from 13. At 35 make a crossing with plaits from 34 and 15/16.

The flower centre (Fig. 125b) Makes leaves J, K and L from 35, 25 and 26. Work a six plait crossing into pin 36. The left hand pairs are used to make leaf M but the other four pairs must not be used at this stage. Leaf M and plait from 35 make a crossing at 37. The left hand plait from 37 and the plait from 34 cross at 38. Plait the left hand pairs as far as 39, but do not put up a pin.

The scallop weaver is on the far left, and works as in the previous scallop, using the

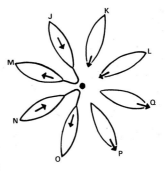

Fig. 125b

twisted pair at 33 and the pairs from the plait as passives. Work * to ** as far as 52. The pairs from 51 are plaited to make a crossing at 53 with the plait from 38. Plaits from 37 and 53 make a crossing at 54. The right hand pairs at 54 make leaf N back towards the flower centre. Remove pin 36. The two leaf pairs and the four pairs left hanging at 36 make a six plait crossing as tightly as possible, and pin 36 is returned to position at the appropriate stage of the crossing working. Work three leaves O, P and Q out from the crossing.

Summary of the flower centre working Make leaves J, K and L, and a six plait crossing. Take the left hand pairs to make leaf M which is used in the scallop, and returns as leaf N. Remove the pin, and repeat the six plait crossing using leaf N and the four hanging pairs. Make leaves O, P and Q.

The left hand leaf and the plait from 54 cross at 55, and plaits from 53 and 55 cross at 56. At 52 the left hand pair is weaver and the third scallop can be worked in the same manner as the others. Note that the weaver returns to the outside edge at the end of the scallop at x, but there is no pin. The plait from 27 and the right hand leaf Q cross at 62, and a plait from 62 and the middle leaf P cross at 63.

The corner (Fig. 126) Note the following points:

On the footside the weavers from j and i cross normally. Pin k is worked linking in the plait, and the weaver returns through its passive pair. Pin 1 is worked, and both pairs remain at the corner until the pillow has been turned. The inner corner pin m is worked using the left hand passive to link in the plait, work the plait out from the corner, and leave the passive hanging freely again to the right of the plait. Pin n cannot be worked until the corner is complete. When leaf w has been worked, and the plait worked to n, take the weaver from k – this should hang as third pair from the outside edge. Work to the left through the passive in cloth stitch and twist, link in the plait at pin n, and take the weaver back through plait and passive to cross with the weaver from the corner at 1.

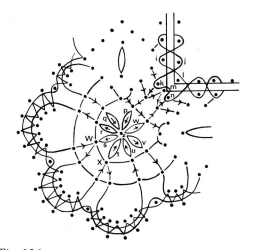

Fig. 126

The flower requires the addition of two pairs extra. Work leaves p and q, use these pairs together with two pairs extra supported on a pin to the left of the centre, and work a six plait crossing. Remove the support pin, and ease the newly introduced pairs to the centre. Leave the right hand two pairs hanging, and make leaves r and s. Take leaf r out and into the scallop, and back to W, where a six plait crossing is made using these plaited pairs, the centre plait and leaf s. Take the left hand pairs, plait them into the scallop, and back to X. Use the other four pairs to make a thick plait to X, and then make a six plait crossing using the same pairs as at W. The left hand pairs make another scallop, and the right hand pairs make leaf t. When the scallop is complete, make leaf u. To complete the centre there are six pairs available, two from u, two from t, and two hanging in the middle at Z. Remove pin Z, and make the crossing, replacing the pin at the correct stage in the working. Turn the pillow. Use the left hand pairs to make leaf v and the right hand pairs to make leaf w. The two centre pairs are knotted together and discarded.

CLUNY PATTERN

Requirements: Twenty pairs of bobbins,. Bockens linen no. 90. Refer to Figs 127 and 128. Prepare pricking 129.

Fig. 127

The footside Hang two pairs round pin a, introduce two passive pairs and work to d.

The trail Place a weaver round pin e, introduce three passive pairs and work to h, Twist both weavers and cross them with cloth stitch and twist.

The headside Hang two pairs round pin k and cover the pin with cloth stitch and twist.

The half stitch oval Hang two pairs round pin m and cover with half stitch. The right side pair becomes weaver and works in letter order. Add single pairs at n and o and two pairs at each of p and q. Nothing is added at r and s, and the weaver works cloth stitch and twist either side of these pins. Add two pairs at pin t, and at u work cloth stitch and twist with the right hand pair from k. At v the weaver crosses with the weaver from j. Work cloth stitch and

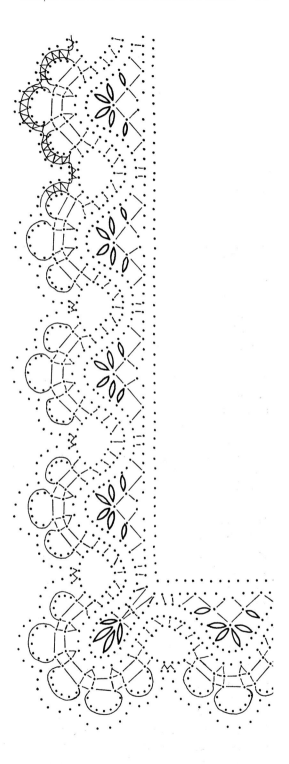

Fig. 129

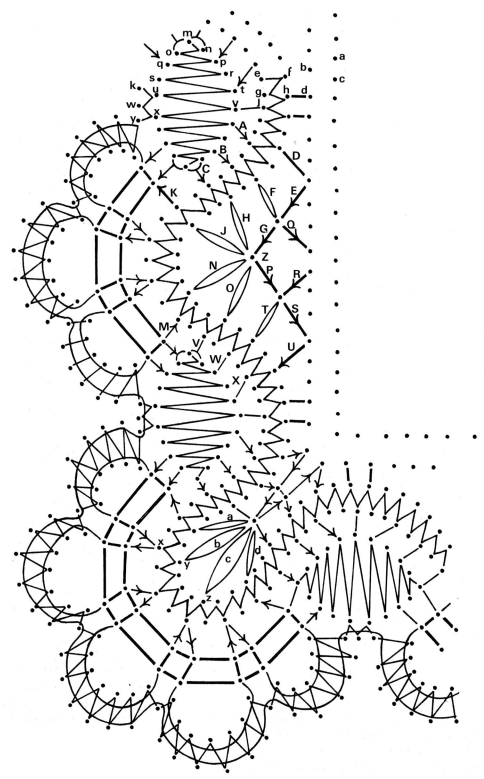

Fig. 128

twist with the outer pair at w, work x as u, and y as w. Complete the oval.

Plaits and leaves Refer to Fig. 121 for the method of taking pairs through the trail. Continue the trail, footside and head as necessary and work plaits and leaves in letter order.

Crossing Z Pairs from G and H make a four plait crossing. Leaf J provides pairs for the scallops and returns from plait M as leaf N. Remove pin Z, the pairs waiting at Z and pairs from N work a four plait crossing and Z is replaced.

The corner Two leaves, a and b, are made from the centre crossing, a provides pairs for the scallops and later returns as d. Leaf b is decoration to fill the space and the pairs become part of the trail, the weaver from x travelling through five pairs to y. After z these pairs are left out for leaf c. At the crossing a small hook is used to join in the leaf pairs, refer to page 177.

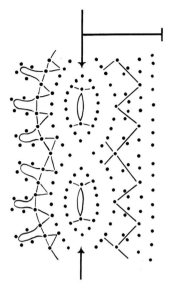

Fig. 130a

Insertions and decorations

Many patterns can be adapted easily to make an insertion or a decoration with two interesting headsides. The uses are many. Insertions may be used to complement the edgings on table or bed linen, they add interest to lampshades, or may be used as dress decoration. Fancy braids may be mounted on velvet as chokers, on ribbon for bookmarks, or on dress as an original adornment. Mounted under glass this lace makes attractive door plates and decorative plaques.

To prepare the pattern (Fig. 130) Use a straight-sided mirror on the centre line of the lace to assess the appearance of the finished insertion.

Place two pieces of paper under the pricking and prick from the footside to the centre line and include the centre pin holes. Place one piece of pricked paper on a pricking board, cut the other piece of paper close to the centre

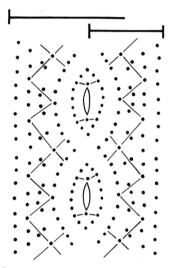

Fig. 130b

holes. Overlap the papers to match the centre holes exactly, place pins in to set the position. Fasten the papers together with sellotape, remove the pins and make a pricking on card.

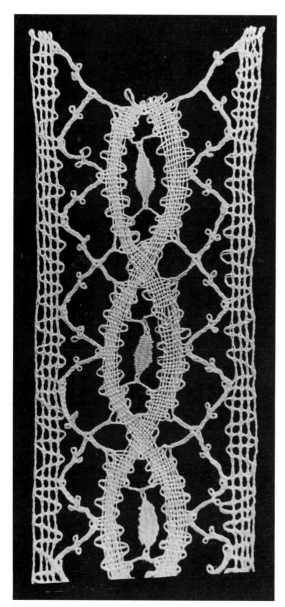

Fig. 131

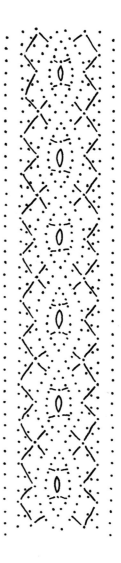

Fig. 132

CROSSING TRAILS AND LEAF INSERTION

Requirements: Twenty-six pairs of bobbins, Madeira Tanne no. 30. Refer to Figs 131 and 132.

The method of working is the same as for the edging on page 66.

DIAMOND AND DAISY INSERTION

Requirements: Twenty pairs of bobbins, DMC Broder Machine Cotton no. 30. Refer to Fig. 133. Prepare pricking 134.

As there are no scallops the working is different from the edging. Four plaits work through to the centre as leaves to make an eight plait crossing. The leaves on the diamond are an optional decoration. The lower part of the lace in the photograph has a normal footside. This can be worked easily when the footside holes are moved to alternate with those on the inner row.

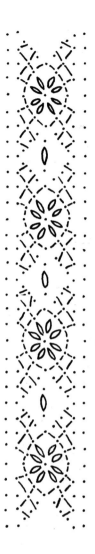

Fig. 134

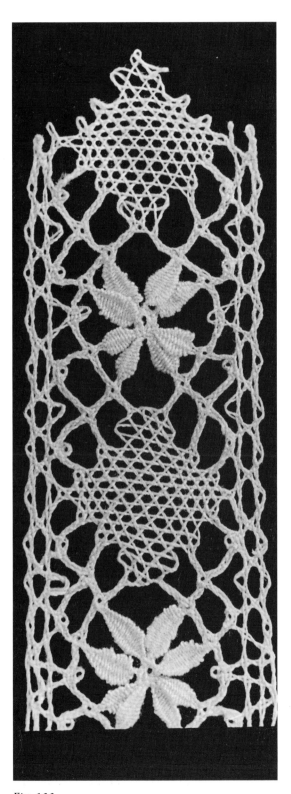

Fig. 133

Eight plait crossing (Fig. 135) Use the four plaits as eight pairs, using each pair as if a single bobbin. Use the centre four pairs to work a half stitch. Make a half stitch with the right hand four pairs and then with the left hand four pairs.

Return to the centre four pairs and work a half stitch. With the right four pairs work a half stitch, and then with the left four pairs. Put up a pin in the centre. Make a cloth stitch with the centre four pairs. Find the right hand four pairs, and cross the centre pairs left over right. Find the left hand four pairs, and cross the centre pairs left over right.

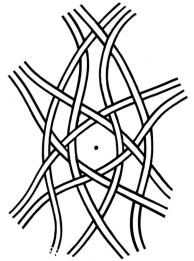

Fig. 135

DIAMOND AND DAISY DECORATION

Requirements: Sixteen pairs of bobbins, DMC Broder Machine no. 30. Refer to Figs 137 and 138. Prepare pricking 139.

This is an adaptation of the edging on page 00. Figs 136a and 136b show the method of achieving the pricking.

To begin, place two pairs of bobbins across the pillow, and put up pin a below the threads. These pairs will become the scallop weavers. Lay six pairs across the pillow below the pin. These will be the passive threads in the scallop edging. Take the extreme left hand two bobbins and weave to the front through three pairs – the first pair in cloth stitch and twist, and the other two pairs in cloth stitch. Put up pin b to the left of the weaver, and weave back to c – through two pairs in cloth stitch, and, having twisted the weaver once, through the last pair in cloth stitch and twist. Put up pin c to the right of the weaver, and continue until pin g is covered with cloth stitch and twist. Take the extreme right hand pair, and weave to the left through three pairs for the other side of the scallop. complete this side as far as s.

The pairs from f and r plait into the pattern. Lay four pairs diagonally across the pillow to make a four plait crossing at z – this method

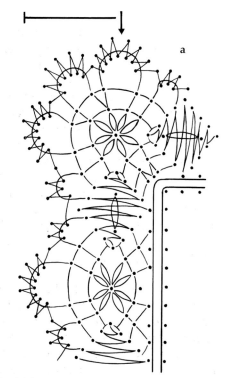

Fig. 136a

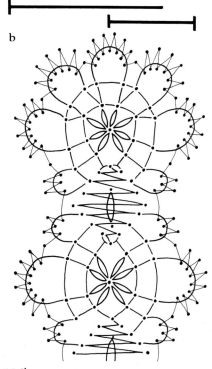

Fig. 136b

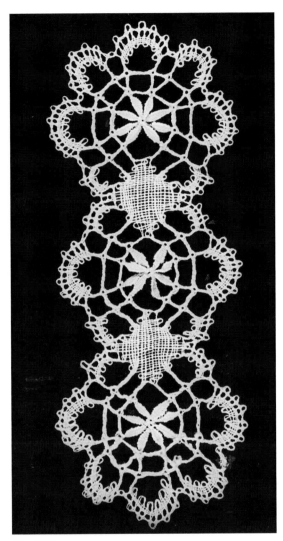

Fig. 137

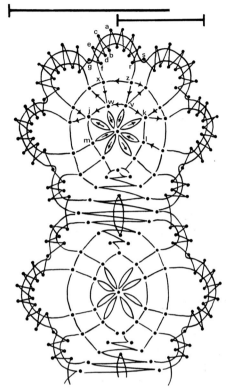

Fig. 138

was described on page 60. Plait to the left to another four plait crossing at x, also plait as far as v. Again lay four pairs diagonally to make a four plait crossing at v, make the three plaits, but temporarily ignore the leaf as there are no available pairs to work it. With the right hand plait from x, and the left hand plait from v, make a four plait crossing at w. Plait both sets of pairs, but ignore the leaf as there are no available pairs to work it. Continue working as far as j and k.

Two pairs must be joined in as follows: remove pin v and pass a crochet hook through the hole to pull through two threads from fresh

pairs. Pass one end of each pair through the loop, and pull up tightly. Replace the pin. Add two pairs at w in the same way, and make leaves to the centre hole. Work a four plait crossing, and make leaves to j and k. At j and k, work six plait crossings, and on each side take out one plait to make the scallop. The remaining eight threads are plaited together as far as l and m, then four are discarded.

Alternatively the leaves may be knotted out at j and k. The leaves from m and l are hooked into the centre crossing, and then more leaves are made to complete the eight leaf centre. The pattern can be worked in the same way as the heading of the strip pattern.

To complete the pattern (Fig. 140) Work leaves a and b together in a four plait crossing in the centre, and make leaves c and d. Work as far as J and S. On the right hand side at J, make the usual four plait crossing, and make leaf e with the left hand pairs. On the left side work similarly, making leaf f with the two right hand

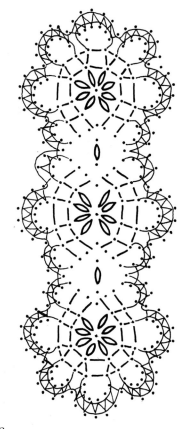

Fig. 139

pairs. Remove the centre pin and link these leaves into the centre. Replace the pin and make leaves g and h. On the right hand side at the end of leaf g, put up pin K, and cover with cloth stitch and twist. Using the *same threads*, plait as far as J. Remove the pin at J, and make

a four plait crossing with the pairs hanging at J. Replace the pin. Knot and discard the right hand pairs.

Plait the left hand pairs for use in the scallop. At the end of the scallop, work the crossing at m, and plait to K. Hook the plait into K, and plait back to n for the next scallop. Work round to O, and then to p. On the left hand side put up pin p at the end of leaf h (there is no crossing), and plait to S. Remove pin S, work a four plait crossing and replace the pin. The left hand pairs are knotted out, and the right hand pairs continue through t and round the scallop to u and p. Join the plaits from u and O into pin p, and plait the eight threads to pin K. Knot firmly and cut off. The weavers and outside pairs of the scallops must be knotted and oversewn at W. The plaits from u and n must be worked to O and knotted off.

To assist the worker, capital letters have been used to indicate the points where threads are knotted out. The path of the plaits will be seen clearly in Fig. 140b.

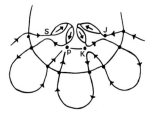

Fig. 140b

Medallions

These are useful to mount under glass paperweights, in the base of small dishes, or for decorative mounting or insertion. The simple designs are most effective, and the worker may design original motifs very easily. There are several ways of working a circular motif, but many designs can be made by starting on a line radiating from the centre and working in a circular direction to finish on the same line. This is straightforward, easy to understand, and requires comparatively few bobbins.

Fig. 140a

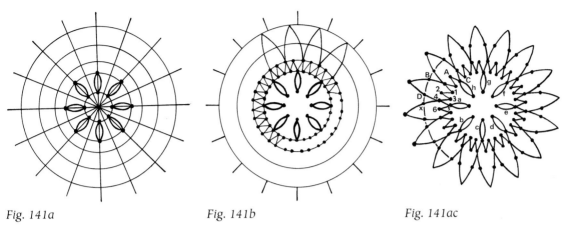

Fig. 141a   Fig. 141b   Fig. 141ac

To plan a circular motif (Figs 141a, 141b and 141c) A very simple example is described here. Decide on the diameter, and draw a circle, inside which all holes must fall. Mark in the radiating lines according to the design envisaged. Eight is a good number to begin a simple pattern. Draw in concentric circles to suit the design planned. Mark in eight leaves around the centre circle. Add radiating lines between those already in use. By 'eye' put three dots between each leaf, and these and the points of the leaves represent pin holes. Mark in the path of a weaver in a circular trail. Add the ninepin edging.

BEDFORDSHIRE MOTIF

Requirements: Fifteen pairs of bobbins, Madeira Tanne no. 30. Refer to Figs 141c and 142. Prepare pricking 143.

Hang two pairs of bobbins on A and one pair on pin 1 as a weaver. Weave in cloth stitch to the left through the pairs on A, and put up pin 2 to the right of the weaver. Weave back to pin 3, and remove support pin A. Hang two pairs on B. Take the weaver at pin 3, and weave to the left through the trail pairs, and through the pairs on B. Put up pin 4 to the right of the weaver. Weave back through the two pairs from B, which will be released for the ninepin, through the two trail pairs, and through two pairs hung on a pin at C. Put up pin 5. Weave to the left through the pairs from C, these being left out to make a leaf in the centre, and

Fig. 142

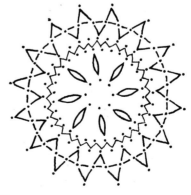

Fig. 143

through the trail pairs. Put up pin 6. Remove support pins B and C.

Plait the pairs left out at pin 4 for the ninepin, and work a four plait crossing with pairs hung on at D into pin x. Continue the trail and ninepin introducing fresh pairs for leaves b, c and d in the same way that pairs were introduced at pin 5 for leaf a.

Work each leaf and complete it with a cloth stitch. Do not put up the pins yet. In order to retain the shape of the leaf the weaver should be supported. At the end of each leaf take the weaver, and place it back over the work so that the weight of the bobbin is falling in the opposite direction from the other three threads.

The centre (Fig. 144) Take the right hand pair of leaf c, weave in half stitch to the right through the two pairs of leaf b, and put up pin s to the left of the weaver. Weave back through these two pairs and through the other half of leaf c, and put up pin t to the right of the weaver. Weave back through these three pairs and the two pairs from leaf a, and put up pin u. Weave through the five pairs and the two from leaf d, and put up pin v. Weave through all seven pairs, and put up pin w, and back through the seven again to put up pin x. Weave through five pairs to y – two pairs are left out for the leaf at w. Weave through three pairs to z – two pairs are left out for the leaf at x. Cover pin z with half stitch, and these two pairs make the leaf from z. The other two pairs make the leaf from y. Make the four leaves.

Push the pins in the completed half of the medallion right into the pillow, and slide a piece of clear plastic over the pin heads. The cover cloths will hold it in position.

Work the second half of the medallion. To bring a leaf into the trail, weave it in, using the trail weaver, put up the pin and weave back through it. Knot the pairs together, and lay the threads back across the work away from the working area. They will be cut off later. Complete the trail and ninepin, and end off neatly.

CLUNY MOTIF

> *Requirements:* Sixteen pairs of bobbins, Madeira Tanne no. 30. Refer to Figs 145 and 146 and prepare pricking 147.

Reference to the Cluny patterns on pages 76 and 81 will facilitate the working of this motif.

The circular cloth trail Hang one weaver pair on A, five pairs on B, and two pairs on C. Weave from A to b through seven pairs and back to c through five pairs. Return through three pairs to d. Continue the trail to g. Remove the support pins B and C.

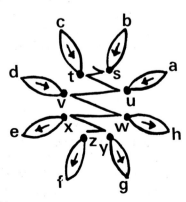

Fig. 144

Fig. 145

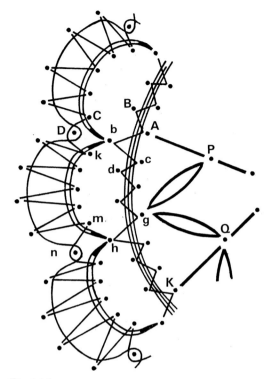

Fig. 146

Fig. 147

Plaits are made from the centre out to the crossings. Each plait is taken into the trail with cloth stitch, and trail pairs are discarded to maintain three pairs throughout.

Collars

Leaves and Plaits Plait from A to P. Hang two pairs round a support pin and introduce them at a four plait crossing at P. Make a leaf and link it into the trail with the weaver at g.

The scallop edge Hang two pairs round D, twist the right side threads three times and cover with cloth stitch and twist. The right hand pair is the weaver and work in cloth stitch through the pairs from the short plait (b to k). Work the scallop to m and n. Make a short plait to h, and the weaver at g works through the trail and links the plait into the trail at h. Work the next scallop.

To continue Introduce two pairs for a plait from K and make crossing Q with this plait and a leaf from g. When a third plait has been introduced, work the centre.

The centre Plait from the crossings to the centre ring. Take a gimp thread through each pair and twist each twice to enclose the gimp. Refer to the previous pattern for method.

A collar should suit and fit a particular garment. Many of the attractive old collar patterns require alteration for modern use. Either the style is not in keeping with present day fashion, or the collar does not fit. Almost all collars from the Victorian period need enlarging, and this is rarely an easy exercise. Today, many dresses have a centre back zip fastener, and collars made in two pieces are needed. These are infrequently found among old patterns unless intended for a dress with a deep V neckline. Many hours of work are spent in making a lace collar and so it is worth the time to plan a collar that will fit and enhance the dress for which it is intended.

To make a pattern (Figs 148, 149 and 150) Use the commercial pattern or the actual garment to obtain the shape and neck edge required. If using the pattern, trim the seam allowance from the neck edge, and fasten the front and back pieces together, matching the shoulder seam line. Place over a sheet of paper and mark in the neck curve, the centre front and

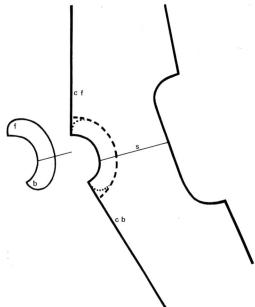

Fig. 148

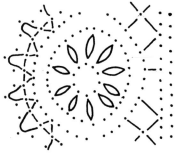

Fig. 149

centre back lines, and the line of the shoulder seam. Cut out the shape and use it to make the collar pattern (Fig. 148). Measure an even distance from the neck edge for the collar width, and mark in a slight curve at back and front. Cut out the collar pattern.

Choose a simple edging (Fig. 149). Select one repeat that is accurate, and prick this through eight pieces of paper, putting the

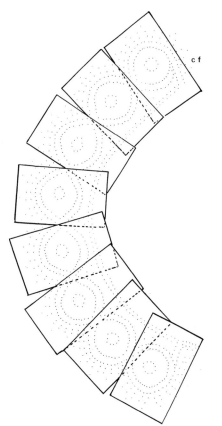

Fig. 150a

Fig. 150b

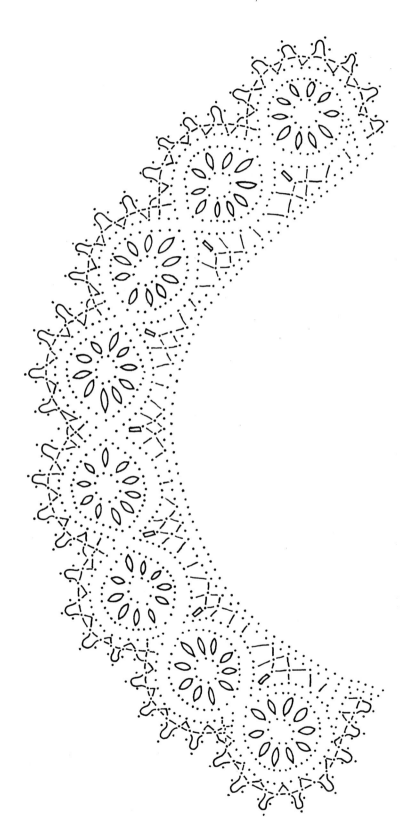

Fig. 152

markings on each piece. Draw an outline of the collar on a sheet of paper, and indicate the front and back. Place the pattern repeats over the collar outline. Overlapping will be necessary near the footside and the arrangement of plaits will require adjustment. Similarly, the ninepin edge will need attention. If the collar outline is pinned over a pricking board it will be easy to move the repeats, temporarily fixing them with pins. (Fig. 150a).

The centre back and front require adaptation and some redesigning. The holes on the neck edge will be a smooth curve and the crossing of trails will need attention. It is a good idea to mark in the weaver to ensure accuracy.

A BEDFORDSHIRE COLLAR

Requirements: Bobbins as required, approximately 30 pairs, 120/2 linen thread. Refer to Fig. 151. Prepare pricking 152.

Place a sheet of plain paper between card and copy when making the pricking. In the past the lacemaker would turn the pricking over and work on the 'rough' side to make the second half. However, today it is prepared by placing the paper copy underside uppermost over card and repricking. The pricking can be enlarged (x 112%) for use with Fresia 100/2 linen thread.

To begin (Figs 153a, 154 and 155) Put up pin A and lay two pairs of bobbins vertically either side of the pin. Enclose the pin with cloth stitch and twist. To do this, work a cloth stitch and twist with the four hanging threads, and then turn the pillow to make a similar stitch behind the pin. Put up pin a to the right of the threads already on the pillow, and hang two pairs on pin a. Using the left hand pair from a, weave in cloth stitch through the two hanging pairs to the left. Take the right hand pair from a, and weave to the left through the same two pairs. The two pairs from a will be passive pairs round the headside trail. The pairs hanging become part of the footside, the left hand pair as a passive, and the right hand pair as one of the footside weavers.

Fig. 151

Allow the pairs from pin a to lie horizontally across the pillow and, ignoring them, place pin b below them. Put two pairs vertically either side of pin b and enclose with cloth stitch as at pin A. Refer to diagram 155 for the use of these pairs. Work in cloth stitch to the footside edge, twist the weaver twice, and work cloth stitch and twist with the edge pair. Put up pin c and return to d. Work cloth stitch through the trail to pin h. Continue, joining in two pairs at j for the ninepin plait. Work the ninepin as required. At the first crossing of plaits, which is at g, use the pairs joined in at j, and the plait from A. Work the curved headside trail joining in one pair at each of pins r, s, t and u; these are left out immediately for the curved right side trail. Join in two pairs at pins v, w, x and y, and leave out immediately.

Return the pillow to the normal working position and use these pairs as follows. Begin the curved right trail by twisting pairs from r, s, t, u and v twice each. Take the left pair from v, and weave to the right through two pairs (i.e. the other pair from v and one pair from u), it

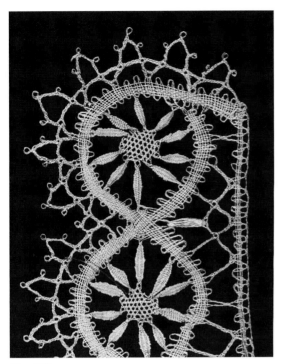

Fig. 153a

Fig. 153b

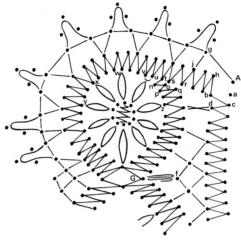

Fig. 154

will be the left hand passive in this trail. The pair from t becomes the trail weaver, and weaves in cloth stitch through one pair to the left, and pin n is put up. The same weaver works to the right through the one passive pair, and through the pair from s. Pin o is put up, and the weaver goes back to the left through two passives to pin p. Weave back to the right through the two passives and the pair from r, put up pin q, and continue the trail with these three passives.

Two pairs must be joined in for a leaf at z. Leaves are made using pairs from w, x, y and z. The other leaf is made with a pair from v and one from u. A pin is put up at the top of the half stitch circle between the pairs of the centre leaf. It is covered with half stitch, and the right hand pair becomes the weaver, weav-

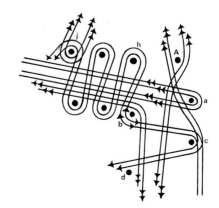

Fig. 155

ing to the right to work in the complete leaf from u/v. Continue weaving and bring in two leaf pairs at each pin, until there are ten pairs (nine and the weaver pair) in the circle. Complete the circle, leaving out pairs as indicated in the diagram. The other five leaves are worked, the trails completed, and a crossing of trails worked. The leaves on the left will join the curved trail, and the leaves on the right will pass through the trail to make plaits. Refer to Fig. 121 (see page 00).

The plaits are worked into the footside normally, and four plait crossings made when required. The plait is worked to pin f, which is put up between the plait pairs. The left hand pair of the plait and the trail crossing weaver from G make a tally. This tally is difficult to manage as the plait is not secure and it is helpful to pin the necks of the bobbins of the other half of the plait firmly by the thread while the tally is being made. The tally weaver is taken to the left, and twisted with the left thread of the tally. The centre and right threads are twisted and used to continue the plait from f.

To complete the collar neatly (Fig. 156) Work the right hand trail as far as a. Work the left hand trail all the way to o; the last leaf to be brought in comes in at b. If all the pins are pressed into the pillow and the bobbins from the other trail laid to the left, this is straightforward to work. At o, the trail weaver links with the weaver from the footside, it then works to p. Cross the pairs on the footside (i.e. two passives and two weavers through the pairs from

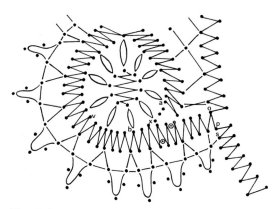

Fig. 156

the headside trail). Take the weaver from the left of pin p, and weave a strip of cloth for approximately one inch, using the four pairs from the footside edge as passives. Tie the bobbins together in pairs, and cut off. The pairs from the trail that passed out to the right hand edge must be tied and cut off.

Press all pins into the pillow, and return to the curved right side trail. With the weaver as at pin a, continue the trail using the ringed pin-holes. Pins will be replaced through the worked trail to these holes. Raise the pins as they are required for use, and work over the other trail as far as v. The last leaf is joined in at x, and then the trail is a simple cloth strip. Knot the ends and cut off. Tuck in the ends and any plait threads, overlap the trails, and sew together. On the footside, turn in the knots, fold the inch strip back to enclose the knots, and sew down.

To make the second half of the collar Work the lace from the centre front, the footside (neck edge) will be on the left. Refer to Fig. 153b.

A CLUNY COLLAR

Requirements: Twenty pairs of bobbins, Bockens linen no. 90. Refer to Fig. 157. Prepare pricking 158. The pricking for the second half of the collar is prepared as described previously.

To begin (Figs 159b and 160) Instructions are given for the collar half with the footside (neck edge) on the left. Hang eight pairs round B. Place pin A between second and third threads from left. Threads to the left of pin A become the weaver and work through the remaining six threads to the left of pin B – cloth stitch and twist, cloth stitch, cloth stitch. Place pin b to the left of the weaver. Work the scallop headside to d. Join in two pairs at d, these are left out to become the footside weavers. Continue the trail to pin e but work through all three pairs with cloth stitch, the decorative headside edge is not required after pin d.

Fig. 157

The headside Turn the pillow round, remove
pin B, twist the threads either side of pin A
twice and cover the pin with cloth stitch and
twist. These are the headside passive and
weaver pairs. From b plait the cloth stitch pairs
and introduce pairs for plaits at crossings f and
g. To facilitate this, a support pin may be put
into the pattern at C. Plait to h where the pairs
are linked into the trail.

The centre leaf feature Continue the trail adding
pairs for leaves at e, j and k. At the same time
work the headside as necessary. The leaf from
m is made with the pairs from the scallop.
Work the four leaves and the half stitch circle.
Leaves and plaits are made as indicated.

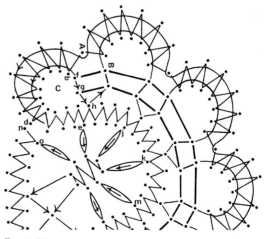

Fig. 160

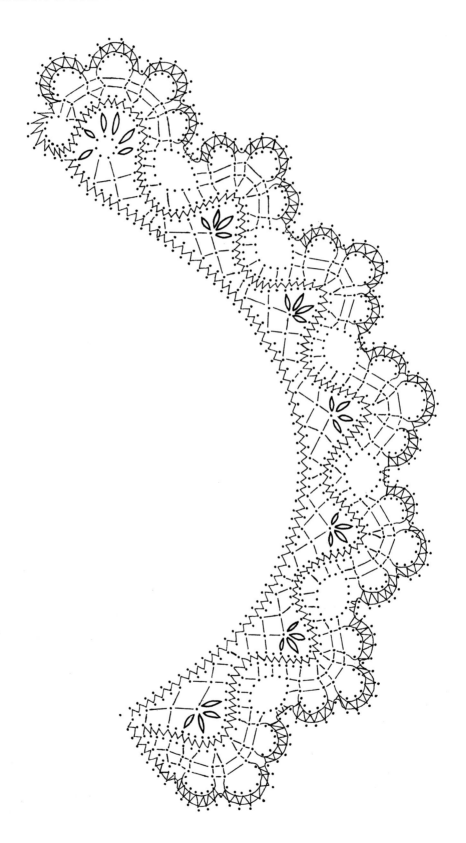

Fig. 158

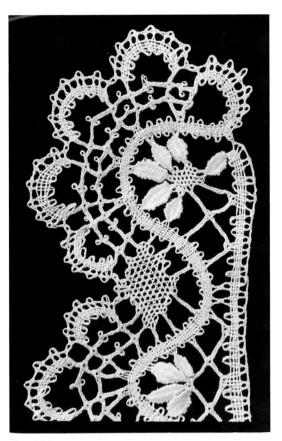

Fig. 159a

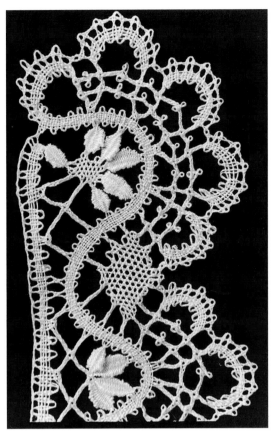

Fig. 159b

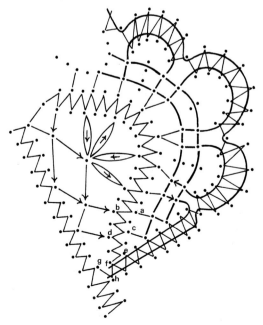

Fig. 162

The footside Twist each pair from d twice, and work cloth stitch and twist. Put pin n to the right of both pairs. Work cloth stitch through the leaf pairs and put pin o to the left of the weaver. Continue the footside with these pairs. The pattern on page 81 is similar.

To complete the collar (Figs 161 and 162) The plait pairs which enter the trail at a, b, c and d are discarded within the cloth stitch. This is achieved as follows: working towards pin a, discard one pair by laying it back out of the trail. Include the two plait pairs at a. Working towards b, discard two more threads, but not plait threads. Continue to discard in every row. These pairs are cut off close to the lace later, it is unnecessary to sew or knot them. The weaver in the outer trail at e works through the weaver from the inner trail and at f all other pairs are taken in. Similarly the footside weaver takes in the trail weaver at g and the

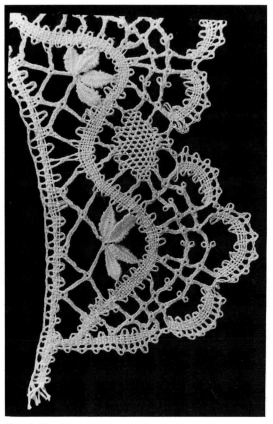

Fig. 161

was worked and a trail travelled continuously round the wing, across the body, round the other wing and finished at the body again. The filling was worked at the same time, so that the trails were uneven.

Either way there were few joins and the result was strong enough to withstand frequent laundering. Today it has become the custom to work the body first. The wing is started at the tip and both sides are worked at the same time. Using this method it is easier to get a balanced plait arrangement within the wing. An understanding of techniques and the ability to adapt these to various situations is necessary for the working of all irregular patterns.

BUTTERFLY NO. 1

Requirements: Ten pairs of bobbins, Madeira Tanne no. 50, one pair of gimp bobbins, Coton Perlé no. 8. Additional pairs are required for the wings. Refer to Figs 163 and 164. Prepare pricking 165.

To work the body This requires ten pairs of bobbins and one gimp pair. Put a pin at the tip of one antenna and hang five pairs on it. Make a cloth stitch with the four right hand threads and twist all the pairs three times each. Take the second pair from the right to the left through two pairs in cloth stitch, twist the weaver three times, and work cloth stitch and three twists on the outside edge. Put up the footside pin inside two pairs and work the length of the antenna with a footside on both sides. Work the other antenna similarly, and the weavers should meet at the centre pin, work cloth stitch and twist, put up the pin and cover it. One pair becomes the passive and the other continues as weaver. Work to the outside edge.

Take a gimp pair and pass it through the seven centre pairs, but not through the weavers. The gimp threads will lie inside the weavers on each side, and will be used as passive threads in the lace. In each case the other half of the pair will be a thin lace thread. The head can be worked in half stitch, and, if desired, a raised tally may be worked in the

remaining trail pairs at h. Discard trail pairs to avoid a very thick trail from h. Work a 20 mm trail and knot the threads together.

Work the second half from centre front with the footside on the right.

Butterflies

Butterflies and flower motifs, found in collections of old Bedfordshire patterns, were used for insertion in household linens. Today, with some adaptation, they are placed under glass in trays or pictures or used independently with a pin for dress decoration. The method of working will depend on the use to which the lace will be put. The traditional lace butterfly was usually started at one wing tip and completed at the other; the body was worked horizontally in the centre. Alternatively the body

Fig. 163

centre. In each row of working the first and last pairs, which include the gimp threads, should be worked in cloth stitch. Twists on weavers are necessary to achieve a neat half stitch before and after these stitches. The body is worked in cloth stitch with a twisted weaver in the centre.

At the end of the body, throw out the gimps, and tie the weavers from each side around all the other threads. Knot the pairs together and tie the weavers around them a second time. Cut off the threads, and rejoin the pairs to begin the wing.

To work the larger wings (Fig. 166) Put up pin c and hang seven pairs on the pin. Work cloth stitch and three twists with the left hand four threads. Twist all the pairs three times, take the second pair from the left and work to the right in cloth stitch through four pairs, twist the weaver three times, and work cloth stitch and three twists on the outside edge. Put up the pin inside two pairs.

Take a gimp pair and place it in position as described for the head. The gimp threads should lie as third from the left and fifth from the right. Continue with footside on both sides,

introducing a new pair at each pin, until there are 11 pairs and the gimp pair.

Join in pairs as follows (Fig. 167), work to the footside through the last passive pair which includes the gimp thread. Put up the footside pin to support the weaver before the stitch is worked, and twist the weaver three times. Put a new pair up and over the weaver, allowing it to fall inside the gimp thread. Complete the footside remembering that the pin is in position but the stitch must be made.

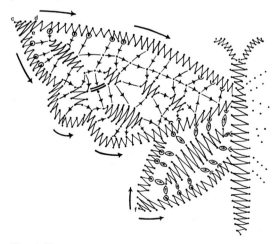

Fig. 164

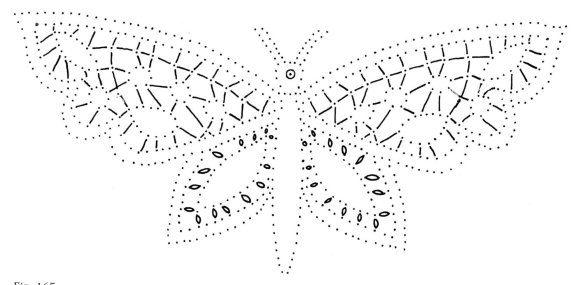

Fig. 165

After pin d, the weaver travels through four pairs only, pin e is put up and covered with cloth stitch and a weaver travels in each direction to continue the edge trails. A ringed hole on the inner edge of the trail indicates that two pairs are joined in at the hole, and a hole capped with a semi-circle indicates that pairs must be discarded at the hole.

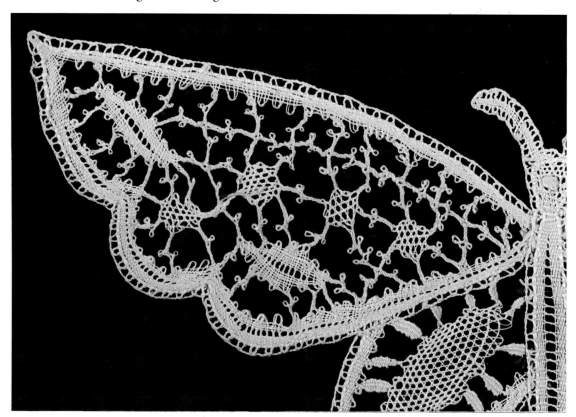

Fig. 166

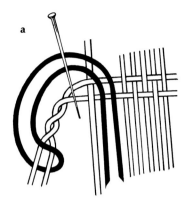

Fig. 167

Fig. 168

To join the edge trail to the body (Fig. 168) remove the pin at the side of the body, and pull one half of the weaver through. Pass the other end of the weaver through the loop, pull them up tightly, and knot them together. Now weave to the other side and join the weaver to the body in the same way. Hook the passive pairs into the edge of the body, make them secure and cut off the threads.

To work the smaller wings The small wing is worked following the photograph and instructions. It is started at pin f with 11 pairs and a gimp pair. One trail is sewn into the body and the other into the lower side of the large wing. Work the other half to match.

BUTTERFLY NO. 2

Requirements: Pairs of bobbins, DMC Broder Machine no. 50, Coton Perlé no. 8. Refer to Fig. 169. Prepare pricking 170.

The body and antennae are worked in the same way as those in the previous pattern.

Working the decorative hole in the body (Fig. 171) Work from the left side towards the centre and right side. Weave through the centre pair and on through one more pair. Ignore the weaver and the pair to the left of it, take the next pair to the left, and work that pair and the next to the left in cloth stitch. These four pairs

make the hole. Twist the inner two pairs three times each, put up a pin between them, and cover with cloth stitch and three twists. The outer pairs work out to the edges of the head, and back to the same position. They are twisted three times each and then worked in cloth stitch through the inner pairs to meet in the middle. Twist all four pairs three times each, and put up pins b and c to the outside of all four pairs. Work the centre pairs in cloth stitch and three twists, and put up pin d below the stitch. The outer pairs work out to the edges of the head and straight back to the centre in cloth stitch. They are worked together in cloth stitch, and one pair is left hanging unsupported while the other becomes the weaver.

The lower wings These are worked first, and the edges completed back to the body. The markings on the pricking indicate the leaf positions. A leaf is made near the point on one side, pairs are joined in for the centre plait, another leaf is made, and the pairs taken into the trail on the other side. The pairs are released for the next leaf. It crosses the centre plait, and another leaf is made and taken into the trail on the other side. Thus the lower wing is worked using very few pairs.

The upper wings (Fig. 172) Place a pin in the hole at the tip of the wing and hang four pairs round the pin. Work cloth stitch and two twists with the threads to the right of the pin. Hang one gimp pair and five pairs round another

Fig. 169

Fig. 170

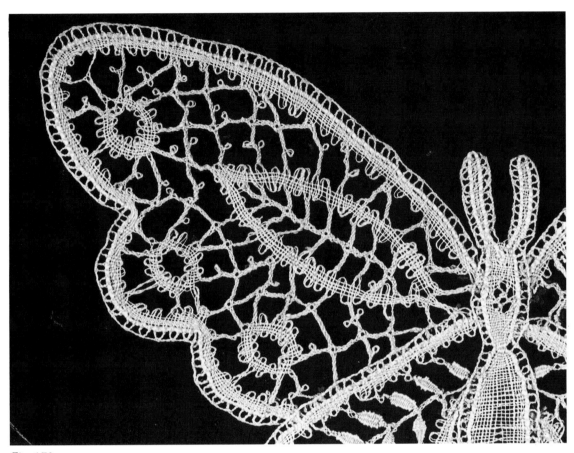

Fig. 172

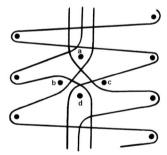

Fig. 171

support pin, these are the passive footside pairs. The inner pairs from the pin at the tip become footside trail weavers. The pairs travel through the oval feature trail as in Cluny lace. The photograph will clarify the method for working the small rings.

If the butterfly is used as a dress trim, make a second body and attach it using a little cotton wool padding in the centre.

Old Bedfordshire patterns

All patterns worked so far are accurate. There are the correct number of holes to weave regular trails, cloth or half stitch solid blocks, and an even footside. Each repeat is identical with the previous one. Old patterns may have been misused and extra holes made or, with years of use, the holes may be enlarged and out of line. Where attention has been given to design, the holes may have been put in position to create the curve required rather than with thought to the way of working. Slight variation in the design is acceptable as it adds to the charm of the hand created article. It is not good to attempt to 'true' every pattern, but it is necessary to improve upon those that are badly out of line.

To 'true' an old pattern Take a photocopy of the pattern, choose a repeat pattern that looks to be accurate, and draw two lines across the strip to isolate it. Using the holes as a guide, draw in the curves accurately and any other important pattern features. Draw a series of curves on the heading in order to space the ninepin, and lightly draw in the position of the plaits. Mark in other plaits and leaves. Use another colour to mark in the weavers in the trails, footside and cloth or half stitch. The pin-hole on one side of a trail, block, or footside should fall actually on the repeat line, as this facilitates the making of a series of repeats into a strip for working. Care must be taken to ensure that the plaits and leaves enter and leave the trails regularly, and that the direction of these is acceptable. The holes on the foot-side should be equidistant.

Place this adjusted photocopy over three sheets of paper, and prick in the holes from the weaver lines. Prick in the other features and the crossings. Other than ninepin do not prick in holes for picots as these can be added later by 'eye'.

Cut along the repeat lines of two of the prickings, and place them carefully in position, one on either side of the third. Mark in plaits, leaves and weavers on the complete strip. If satisfactory, fasten them firmly together, and make a pricking on card.

An alternative method of adjusting a pattern is to measure it up, select a suitable graph paper and work a repeat out accurately. The fine grid helps to achieve even curves and an even footside. Sometimes a short length of the pattern may be better than the rest and repeats of this can be used.

To 'read' a pattern Frequently workers are concerned that they cannot picture the finished lace from a pricking. It is important to study each pricking with its photograph and finished lace to achieve some understanding. The following points will help to interpret the ink markings on prickings:

1   Plaits are marked with straight lines, usually there are picot holes to the side.

Occasionally the picot hole is surrounded by a small ring to indicate on which side the picot falls.

2   The leaf shape denotes the leaf.

3   A short single line between the trail and the footside, or between two trails indicates that the weavers meet and cross. The usual form of crossing of weavers is a 'kiss'. A slightly thicker line indicates that the weavers make a tally. This is frequently found in the heading – leaves are worked in to the centre, back out again, and when the number is uneven a tally is worked at the centre.

4   A small cross in the middle of a block indicates that it is worked in half stitch. Trails are marked with an occasional cross when the working is in half stitch.

5   A circle about a hole in the centre of a block or floral shape denotes a raised tally. This can be seen in the Torchon sampler on page 38.

6   A thick line around any shape indicates the presence of a gimp thread. Half stitch benefits from being enclosed with a gimp, as alone it has untidy edges.

7   Thick lines are sometimes drawn through a trail in order to indicate its position and importance.

8   Patterns with point fillings may have additional markings, but these can be found in the chapter on Bucks Point lace.

TRADITIONAL PATTERN – WITH TALLIES AND LEAF WHEELS

Requirements: Pairs of bobbins as
required, DMC Broder Machine no. 50.
Refer to Fig. 173. Prepare pricking 174.
Refer to the photograph to add the picots.

It is essential to achieve good tension in the
cloth trails and oval to accommodate all the
pairs. Alternatively, pairs may be discarded
and reintroduced but this should not be
necessary.

Fig. 173

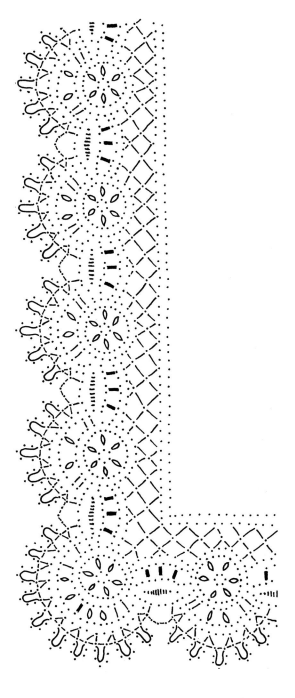

Fig. 174

TRADITIONAL PATTERN – WITH PIN CHAIN AND DOUBLE NINEPIN.

Requirements: Pairs of bobbins as required, Madeira Tanne no. 80. Refer to Fig. 175. Prepare pricking 176.

Instructions for working the filling are on page 148. Fig. 177 explains the working of the double ninepin on the headside.

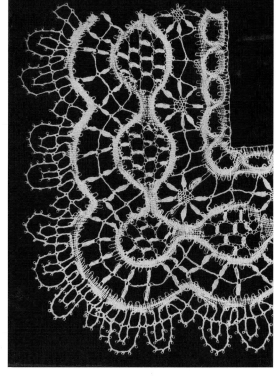

Fig. 175

Fig. 176

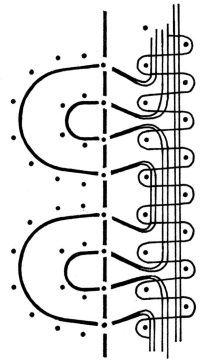

Fig. 177

A CIRCULAR MAT

Interesting features are found frequently in old prickings. The idea for the mat has been taken from an old lappet, a pricking that has little use today.

Requirements: Pairs of bobbins as required, Madeira Tanne no. 50. Refer to Fig. 178. Prepare pricking 179.

Fig. 178

Fig. 179

4. Bucks Point Lace

Bucks Point Lace is an intricate lace recognized by the fine hexagonal net and honeycomb stitches. The net is worked in diagonal lines from the footside into the design which may be a simple shape or an elaborate floral pattern. The fine, closely-woven and twisted threads, the many effects produced by the variety and combination of stitches, together with the use of gimp threads, result in a lace of great beauty. The regular Torchon laces can be imitated readily by machine but the combination of the hexagonal net, the design and picots are still achieved only in the hand-created article.

Explanation of terms and techniques used

Picots Double picots are described on page 50. Single picots are *never* used.

Gimp thread This is always enclosed with twists which may be part of the previous stitch or added as required. Two twists are needed with honeycomb, two with cloth or half stitch, and three with ground. When gimp threads lie together there are no twists between them unless a particular effect is desired, usually only in more elaborate laces. A gimp thread always passes under the left thread and over the right thread of any pair.

Thread In geometric laces the distance apart of holes along the footside edge may be used as a guide.

Holes 2.5 mm (1/10th inch) apart: DMC Broder Machine no. 30, Madeira Tanne 30.

Holes 2.0 mm (1/12th inch) apart: DMC Broder Machine no. 50, Madeira Tanne 50.

Finer patterns require thinner thread, for example Madeira Tanne 80.

More complex patterns usually require the thinner threads, often the ground is coarse in comparison with the rest of the pricking. If in doubt work part of the cloth work and filling to decide on a suitable thread.

Gimp threads: Coton Perlé is most suitable as it is soft and similar in texture to the old linen floss used in the past. No. 8 is used for most work but for very fine patterns with Madeira Tanne 80 a no. 12 is preferable.

To prepare the pricking: As Bucks Point lace is fine it is not easy to achieve an accurate pricking. The ground and fillings in Torchon lace are worked along diagonal lines at 45° from the footside. The angle in Bucks Point lace

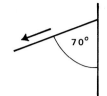

Fig. 180

varies between 52° and 70° according to the design (Fig. 180). Alteration usually has a detrimental effect, changing the shape of the diamonds, fans and flowers.

Geometric designs: Refer to instructions on page 3. A straight headside should be pricked, using a ruler as a guide, in the same way as the footside. Curved picot headsides are put in according to the photocopy. The pricking of floral patterns is discussed on page 146.

Note: Corner instructions have been included with each pattern, but initially the inexperienced lacemaker should work several edgings to understand the fundamental principles. Before attempting a corner, refer to page 152.

FAN PATTERN

Requirements: Thirteen pairs of bobbins, Madeira Tanne no. 30. One single gimp bobbin, Coton Perlé no. 8. One pair extra is needed for the corner. Refer to Figs 181 and 182. Prepare pricking 183. This is a coarse pricking on which to learn.

A more attractive result will be obtained if the pricking is reduced (x 85%) and worked with Madeira Tanne no. 50.

Hang two pairs on A1 and two pairs in order on B. Hang one pair on C to G inclusive, and allow the gimp thread to hang to the left of the pair on pin G. The gimp should be supported on a pin slightly further back than the other support pins. Hang four pairs on H in order from left to right.

To begin Twist the right hand bobbins on A1 three times, and cover pin A1 with cloth stitch

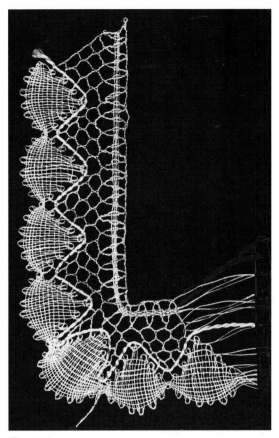

Fig. 181

and three twists. Cloth stitch and three twists is a stitch consisting of cloth stitch and three twists on each pair of bobbins. (Refer to Fig. 12 on page 8 and the sequence is a, b, c, b, b, b.) Ignore the right hand pair and weave to the left through two pairs from B in cloth stitch. Twist the weaver three times, and work a ground stitch with the pair from C.

Ground stitch Using two pairs, cross the second bobbin over the third, and then take the second over the first and the fourth over the third at the same time. Repeat this last move twice more. (Refer to Fig. 12 and the sequence is a, b, b, b.) It is important to think of this stitch as cross and three twists. Put up pin 2 to the right of both pairs. This is known as the catch pin. Take the left hand pair and the next pair, which hangs from D, and work another ground stitch. Put up pin 3 between the pairs.

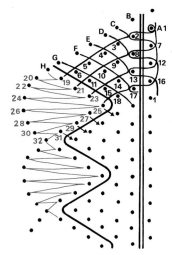

Fig. 182

Do not cover the pin. Take the left hand pair and the pair from E, and work a ground stitch and put up pin 4. Work pin 5 with the pair from F, and pin 6 with the pair from G. If all the ground stitches have been worked accurately with three twists, the extreme left thread will have travelled from the footside pin. Check this by pulling the thread gently, and movement will be seen back to the footside. Remove the support pins C to G. B may be left in position a little longer as it supports the two passive pairs on the footside.

Whenever the footside has to be worked the full sequence is as follows: take the fourth pair from the outside edge, and work cloth stitch through two pairs towards the outside edge. Twist the weaver three times, work cloth stitch and three twists with the outside pair, and put up the pen inside two pairs. (In this case pin 7). Ignore the outside pair and work cloth stitch back through the two passive pairs. Twist the weaver three times.

The catch pin is worked as follows Take the weaver that has completed the footside sequence, and use it and the next pair to make a ground stitch. The catch pin is put up to the side of these pairs, the side nearest the passive pairs (In this case pin 8, to the right of both pairs).

Now take the left hand pair and work the diagonal row and pins 9, 10 and 11. Return to

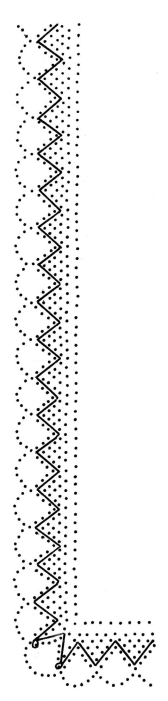

Fig. 183

work footside pin 12 and catch pin 13. Work ground pins 14 and 15. Complete the next row 16, 17 and 18.

Note that rows of ground are *always* worked diagonally. They are worked from a point furthest from, to a point nearer to the worker, and one stitch less has to be worked in each row.

The gimp thread This lies between the cloth fan and the ground. It is passed between the threads of pairs 6, 11, 15 and 18. The gimp thread is always enclosed by twists. The pairs which have completed the ground are twisted already and the gimp is passed under the left thread and over the right. The pairs are twisted twice after the gimp.

To continue Take the left pair from H as weaver and weave in cloth stitch through the other three pairs on H and on through the pair from 6. Put up pin 19 and twist the weaver twice. Weave back through four pairs to the outside edge at pin 20. Twist the weaver twice and work back through five pairs – four already in the fan and the pair from 11. Put up pin 21 and continue to bring in pairs at 23 and 25. From pin 26 work back through six pairs to pin 27. One pair has been left out after pin 25 – the point of the fan. Always keep the same weaver. Work from 28 to 29 through five pairs and from 30 to 31 through four pairs. At pin 32 leave the weaver at the edge and the pin uncovered as it will be easier to find. Twist pairs hanging from 25, 27, 29 and 31 twice and pass the gimp through over the right and under the left thread of each pair. Twist each pair three times to enclose the gimp, they are ready to work the ground. Take the fourth pair from the outside edge and work out to pin 1 for a complete repeat of the pattern.

The corner (Fig. 184) Complete the cloth fan, and work the footside stitch a. Work the catch pin stitch b, and ground stitches c, d and e. Work a footside pin at the corner at pin f and a ground pin at g. The cloth fan weaver is at p.

An extra pair must be introduced into the cloth. Bring one pair up round the weaver and let it fall inside one thread as described in Fig. 167 on page 103. Weave in cloth stitch to the right through four pairs. Pass the gimp thread to the left through the last pair from the fan and through the weaver from the cloth fan (Fig. 185). The weaver and the pair from o are

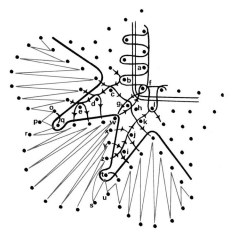

Fig. 184

both to the right of the gimp; work them together in cloth stitch, put up pin q, and cover with cloth stitch. Twist the right hand pair twice, and pass the gimp towards the right through the untwisted weaver and through the twisted passive from o. Take the gimp on to the right through two pairs from e, one pair from d, and one pair from g. Twist all the pairs after the gimp except the weaver. Weave to r, and continue the fan as far as s. Pass the gimp thread to the left through the pairs from w, x, y and z, and on through the next passive pair. Twist this passive pair twice before and twice after the gimp passes through. The fan weaver works from pin s through five pairs and the

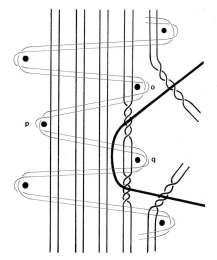

Fig. 185

gimp thread is passed through the untwisted
weaver. The weaver and passive are to the
right of the gimp. Twist the passive and work a
cloth stitch and pin t. Cover pin t and pass the
gimp back to the right through the untwisted
weaver and the passive which is twisted twice
before and twice after the gimp. Weave to u.
Pairs from w, x, y and z must be twisted three
times to enclose the gimp.

The pillow must be turned to work the next
side with the footside on the right. Pairs from
w and g work a ground pin at h, and the footside is worked next using the fourth pair from
the edge, and the corner pin f is used a second
time. The weaver from the corner as usual
passes back through two passive pairs, is
twisted and left waiting for the pair for the
catch pin to be made available. The ground
pins will be worked from the furthest point –
from left to right – until the normal diagonal
line is seen again. Use pairs from y and z to
make a ground stitch, and put up pin i. Take
the right hand pair and the pair from x, and
work a ground stitch into pin j. Use the right
hand pair and pair from h to work k.

Sufficient pairs are available for the next
cloth fan. Pass the gimp through pairs from i, j
and k. The extra pair in the fan should be
removed. Put the penultimate pair of passives
back across the work. Later they may be cut
off. Work the fan completely, and take the
gimp through ready to work the ground.

The first row of ground has the corner pin f
as its footside pin and this has been worked
already. Take the weaver from the footside
which was left in position as fourth pair from
the edge, and work a catch pin with the next
pair to the left. Continue the diagonal row of
ground.

Nook pins The pins at q and t are nook pins;
they occur frequently in floral designs. The
general method of working is as follows: the
weaver is passed round the gimp without twisting in order to keep the lace flat. The passive
pairs are always twisted twice on either side of
the gimp. Refer to Fig. 185.

SHEEP'S HEAD

Requirements: Fifteen pairs of bobbins,
Madeira Tanne no. 50. Four extra pairs
are required for the corner. One pair gimp
bobbins, Coton Perlé no. 8 and one pair
extra for the corner. Refer to Figs 186 and
187. Prepare pricking 188.

This pattern introduces picots on a straight
headside, honeycomb stitch and the use of
gimp threads.

To begin Hang bobbins in the same way as for
the fan pattern. Choose the longest diagonal
row of ground holes, this row has nine holes
and leads into pin 1. At the footside indicate
this row with a pin and hang two pairs of bobbins on it; it is the equivalent of A1. Now put

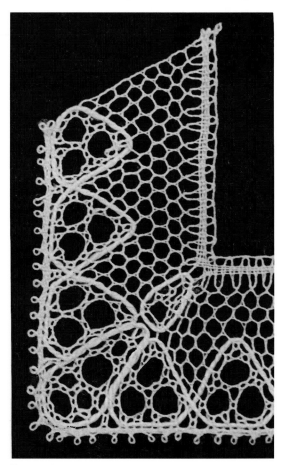

Fig. 186

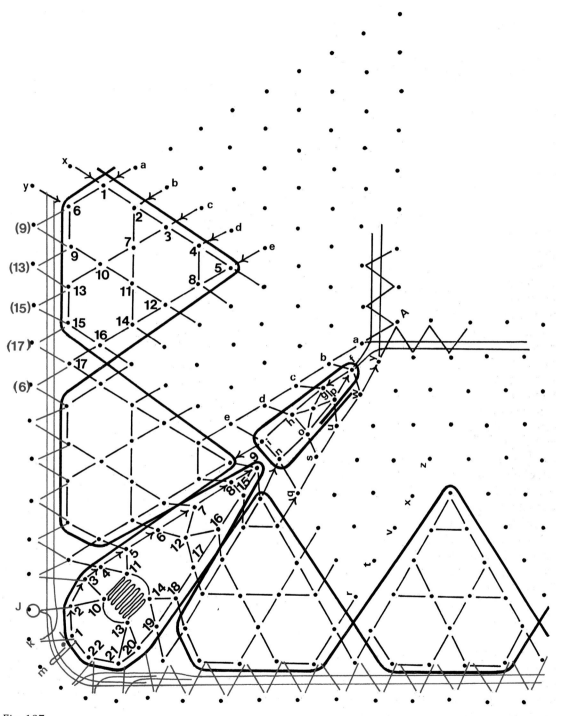

Fig. 187

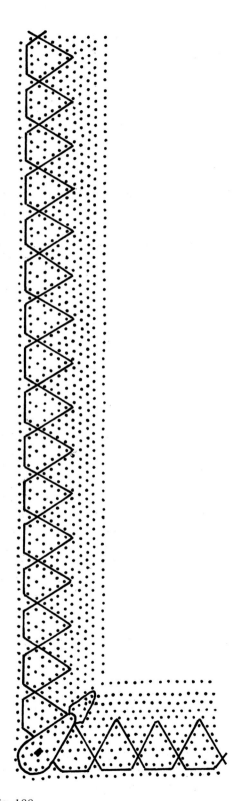

Fig. 188

up pins on the diagonal row *behind* the row to
be worked. On the first pin put up two pairs in
order and one pair on each of the other pins.
Refer to the previous pattern (Fig. 182). The
capital letters refer to support pins and the
numbers refer to order of working.

Work the first row of ground – counting the
footside pin, there are nine pins to be worked.
Remove support pins. Work four more diagonal lines, each one stopping at the black line
which indicates the gimp thread. Pairs should
hang from pins a, b, c, d and e. Hang one pair
on pins X and Y. Take the gimp pair and hang
it on a support pin behind pin 1, and allow
both threads to fall between the threads from a
and X. Take the left hand gimp thread through
pairs from X and Y, and twist the pairs twice
after the gimp. Take the right hand gimp thread
to the right through pairs from a, b, c, d and e.
Twist these pairs twice each.

Honeycomb stitch This is made using two pairs.
Take the second bobbin over the third; and the
fourth over the third and the second over the
first at the same time. Repeat the second
movement. (Refer to Fig. 12: abb). One honeycomb stitch having been made, the pin is put
up and covered with a second honeycomb
stitch. Honeycomb pins are always covered,
and the stitches always have two twists.

Use the pair from a and the pair from X to
make a honeycomb stitch, put up pin 1, and
cover. Use the right hand pair and the next
pair to the right (from b) to work the next honeycomb pin 2. The right hand pair and pair
from c work honeycomb pin 3. The pair from d
is used for pin 4, and from e for pin 5. This row
of honeycomb is continuous from pins 1 to 5.
It is worked diagonally from the point furthest
away to a nearer point. Remove pin X.

Use the pair from 1 and the pair from Y to
work honeycomb pin 6. Use pairs from pins 2
and 3 for pin 7, and pairs from 4 and 5 for pin
8. The row of stitches, 6, 7 and 8 are quite separate. There is a gap between each stitch.
Remove pin Y and ease the thread down.

Pin Y can be replaced and two more pairs
hung on it in order. *Pass the gimp through the
left hand pair from pin 6, twist the pair twice,

and weave to the left through the two passive pairs hung up at Y. Make a double picot into pin 9. For double picots refer to Fig. 78, page 50. Remember that one picot consists of three twists, the threads round the pin, and three more twists. Take the picot pair back through the two passive pairs in cloth stitch, twist twice, pass the gimp through and twist twice more. ** The sequence * to ** is used regularly for each picot pin.

At pin 17 the pair will not travel back through the gimp as that pin is between the two heads.

Take the weaver that has come through from picot (9), and use it and the pair from 6 to work pin 9. Complete the continuous row of honeycomb, pins 10, 11 and 12. The left hand pair from 9 works picot (13). Follow instructions from * to **. On return it works with the pair from pin 10 into pin 13. Pin 14 is the other honeycomb stitch in the gap row. Work picot (15) and the last continuous row of honeycomb at pins 15 and 16.

The honeycomb must be enclosed in gimp, pass the gimp to the left through pairs from 5, 8, 12, 14 and 16. The other gimp goes to the right through pairs from 15 and 16. Cross the gimps right over left. Take the pair from 15 for a picot at (17), and bring the pair back through the two passives but not through the gimp. The left hand pair from 16 works a honeycomb pin with this pair at 17. Make the picot at (6). Remove pin Y and ease the pairs down. One pattern is complete. The pairs at 17 and (6) come in for the next pattern as the pairs did from X and Y.

The corner Work four rows of ground for the honeycomb fan before the corner. The last row is corner pin A, catch pin a and ground stitches b, c, d and e. The pair hanging from a works two cloth stitches to the right through the passive footside pairs and eventually will become a passive on the next side. Pass a gimp thread through pairs from e, d, c, b and the footside passive indicated in the diagram. This pair and the pair from b work honeycomb pin f. continue through g, h and i. The left pair from i passes round both gimps for the point of the fan.

Complete the honeycomb fan.

Cross the gimps and take the right gimp on through the pairs from the fan. The two lie together as one and are enclosed with twists. The other gimp travels to the left through five pairs as follows: the usual two from the headside picots, two from the false picot at j (for false picot see the next pattern) and ordinary picot at k and one which is placed around a pin at l. This pair works to the left to make picot m and returns round the gimp. Work the honeycomb in number order, making the tally before working pin 13. If preferred work the inner pairs from pairs 10 and 11 with a honeycomb pin in place of the tally (see photograph).

Make picots as shown and leave out three pairs. To do this select a pair that has been in the cloth headside trail for some distance and lay it back out of the work. Repeat this until there are two only remaining for the head on the edging.

Work the next honeycomb fan.

Return to the narrow honeycomb feature and work pins n, o, the stitch between pairs from h and g, and pin p. Remove pin f and make the last honeycomb stitch with the pair at f. Replace pin f. The right pair at f passes out round the gimp and works cloth stitch with the next pair.

Complete rows of ground from q to r, s to t, u to v and w to x. Make the ground stitch at y with the right pair from w and remaining passive pair. Place the catch pin to the right of the stitch. Work the row to z. The pair from y is fourth from the edge, it works out to the footside and pin A is used a second time.

SHEEP'S HEAD DECORATION

Requirements: Eighteen pairs of bobbins, Madeira Tanne no. 50. One pair gimp bobbins, Coton Perlé no. 8. Refer to Figs 189 and 190. Prepare pricking 191.

When the Sheep's Head pattern is fully understood, the adaptation to a decorative strip with neat beginning and ending can be practised.

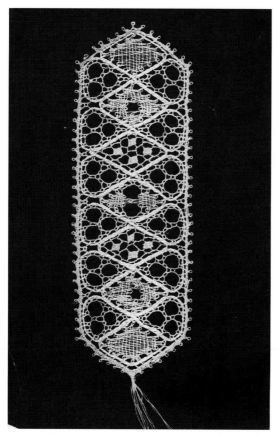

Fig. 189

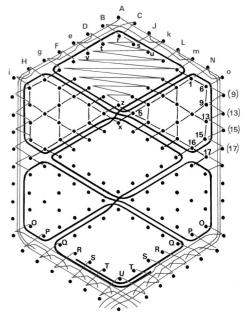

Fig. 190

False picots are necessary to achieve the picot effect when joining in new threads. They are worked as follows: two pairs are hung on a pin, the threads each side of the pin are twisted three times each, and the pin is covered with a cloth stitch. This creates a corded or twisted effect round the pin. It is kept firm by the cloth stitch. Two new pairs are introduced and normally only *one is brought into the work from each picot pin.*

To begin (Fig. 192) Make false picots at B, A and C. Take the left hand pair from A through both pairs from B in cloth stitch. Take the right hand pair from A and work through both pairs from C in cloth stitch. These become outside passives pairs. Work the left pair from C and the right pair from B together to cross them and they become the inner passives. The left hand pair from B works cloth stitch through

one more pair to the right and the right hand pair from C works through one more pair to the left. Twist these pairs twice, pass the gimp thread through and enclose with two more twists. These work cloth stitch, pin r, cloth stitch at the top of the diamond. The left pair hangs as passive and the right pair becomes the weaver.

To work the picots (Fig. 193a) Make a false picot at D, work the right pair through the passive pairs (X and Y), twist it twice, pass the gimp thread through and twist twice more ready for pin t. The remaining pair at D works cloth stitch with the adjoining pair. The third pair (Y) from the edge works out to make the picot at e and returns through the passives (X and Z) for pin v. Continue to make false picots at F and H and ordinary picots at g and i. On the other side (Fig. 193b) make false picots at J, L and N and ordinary picots at k, m and o. Twist pairs and pass the gimp between, twist again.

The cloth diamond Use the right pair at r as weaver and remember to cover pin z with cloth stitch. Twist pairs from the diamond, pass the gimp threads through to cross below z. The left

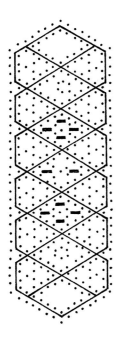

Fig. 191

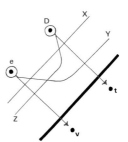

Fig. 193a

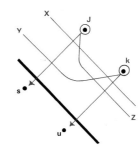

Fig. 193b

gimp remains in this position and the right gimp continues through the five pairs from the right of the diamond, and pairs from N and o. Twist twice in preparation for honeycomb.

The honeycomb head This is worked in the same way as the Sheep's Head although it is on the other side of the lace. Row 1 to 5 is the first row of continuous honeycomb stitches. Rows beginning at 6 and 13 are gap rows, and rows worked from 9 and 15 are continuous. Remember that the picot with the number enclosed in a bracket has to be worked before the honeycomb stitch with the same number. Take the right gimp through both pairs at 16, and to the left through the other four pairs from the head. It crosses the other gimp and continues through pairs from the left side of

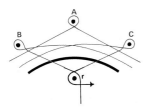

Fig. 192

the cloth diamond, and through pairs from H and i. Complete the Sheep's Head on the left side of the pattern, referring to Fig. 187 if necessary. Take the gimp back to the right to the centre, and cross it under the other gimp above pin x. Take these crossed gimps out in each direction ready for the next diamond.

Diamond fillings A variety of patterns are given in the diamond shapes and choice is at the discretion of the worker.

Cloth diamond with hole (Fig. 194a) Also refer to the Torchon sampler on page 00.

Ground with tallies (Fig. 194b) The method of making tallies or spots is described in the chapter on Torchon on page 00 and basically the method is the same. It is important at the end of a tally that the pair containing the tally weaver should be used only after the other pair, as its immediate use will pull the tally out of shape.

Make ground stitches at a, b, c, d, e and f. Use the left hand pair from f and the right hand pair from b to make a tally. As there are three twists on each pair, the tally should be

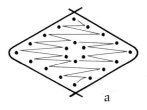 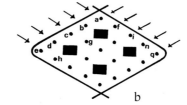 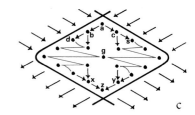

Fig. 194abc

woven straight away, taking the second thread over the third and under the fourth. When completed, the tally weaver should be on the right. Twist the left hand threads and the right hand threads together three times each, and support the weaver in the right hand pair by placing the bobbin horizontally on the pillow until required.

The left hand pair and pair from c work pin g. The left hand pair from g and the pair from d work another tally. The weaver must be left on the right at the end of the tally. The left hand pair from the tally and the right hand pair from e work pin h. The next diagonal row of ground from i is worked normally, and the row beginning with pin n is similar to row f. The last row from q is a normal row.

Honeycomb and cloth (Fig. 194c) Pins a, b and c are honeycomb pins. Cloth diamonds begin at d and s. The diagram shows incoming and outgoing pairs. At g, the weavers work together in cloth stitch, the pin is covered, and the weavers return to their own diamonds. Pins x, y and z are honeycomb pins. Remember to twist twice the pairs coming out of cloth for honeycomb.

To complete the lace Work the last cloth stitch diamond, and enclose it with the gimp threads. Overlap the gimps through three pairs on each side, and allow them to fall back out of the way of working. Later they will be cut off. Both sides are worked in the same way. Starting at O, take the pair out to do a picot and back through two pairs. Take the pair from P out to make a picot and back through two pairs. Discard the last pair worked through (i.e. the second passive from the picot edge).

Take pairs out from Q, R, S, T and U and discard one pair each time. When both sides have been worked, there will be three pairs hanging on each side – pass them directly through each other in cloth stitch so that they lie very flat. Take the outside pairs and cross them under the centre pairs, bring them round to the top, and tie them together tightly. Tie each pair of bobbins in the centre, then take the outside threads round the bundle once more, and tie. Trim all threads to leave a tassle.

CHURCH WINDOW

Requirements: Eighteen pairs of bobbins, Madeira Tanne no. 50. One pair gimp bobbins, Coton Perlé no. 8. An additional two pairs and two gimp pairs are needed for the corner. Refer to Figs 195 and 196. Prepare pricking 197.

To begin the pattern Select the longest row of ground stitches and put up the footside pin with two pairs on it ready to begin. This row has a footside pin, catch pin, seven more ground pins, and ends at a (nine pins altogether). On the row behind hang up pairs on support pins. If necessary refer to the instructions for the Fan pattern, page 111. Work seven rows of ground, ending at pins a, b, c, d, e, f and g. Hang a gimp pair on A, two pairs on each of B and C, and two pairs in order on D. Take the right hand gimp through pairs from a, b, c and d and the left hand gimp through pairs from B and C. Twist all pairs twice. When working the honeycomb head, note that all pins with brackets are worked before the same number pin without brackets.

Take the right hand pair from B and the pair from a to work pin 1, complete the continuous

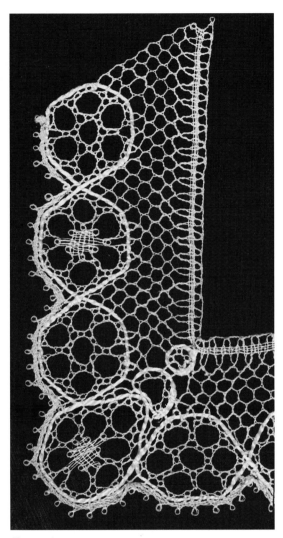

Fig. 195

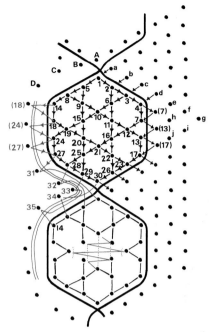

Fig. 196

Before working pin 17 ground pins i (with pairs from g and h), j (with pairs from (13) and i), and (17) (with pairs from 13 and j) must be completed. Remove support pin C.

To begin the picot heading Take the left hand pair from 14, pass the gimp through, twist twice, work two cloth stitches, and make the picot at (18). Bring it back to work pin 18, and then complete the continuous row. From pin 18 the left hand pair works picot pin (24), and then pin 24. Complete the gap row with pins 25 and 26. The left hand pair from 24 works picot pin (27), and then pin 27. Complete the continuous row. Note that there are three picots worked with pairs taken from and returned to the honeycomb head. Enclose the head with gimp, crossing the threads below pin 30.

When working picots, the passive threads should lie flat in the curve and there should be no ugly hole at the deepest point. Work as follows: Pairs hang from 27, 28, 29 and the left hand pair from pin 30. Take the pair from 27 to picot pin 31, and back through two passive pairs only. In turn take pairs from 28, 29 and 30 to work picot pins 32, 33 and 34. The pair

row with 2, 3 and 4. Pairs from B and 1 work pin 5, and from 2 and 3 work pin 6. The gimp passes through the right hand pair from 4 which is twisted three times and makes ground stitch (7) with the pair from e. The gimp passes to the left through the same pair which works pin 7 with the pair from 4. This completes the gap row. Remove support pin B. The right hand pair from C and the left hand pair from 5 work pin 8. Complete the continuous row as far as pin 13. Before pin 13 can be worked, work ground pin h using pairs from 7 and f, and ground pin (13) with pairs from 7 and h. Work the gap row and pins 14, 15, 16 and 17.

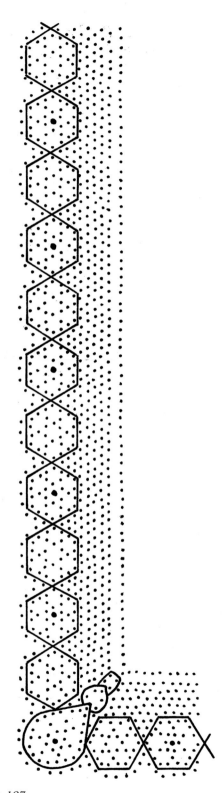

Fig. 197

from 30 works picot pin 34, which is beyond the point, and return through two pairs. Hold this pair and count up the number of picots that introduce pairs into the head which are still to be worked. In this pattern only one pin still has to be worked. Take the pair being held, and work through one more pair in cloth stitch. This pair and the two passives to the right of it pass round the gimp for use in the head. This will leave three passives. The third from the edge passes out through the other two pairs, works picot pin 35, and returns through the passives and round the gimp into the head. A complete pattern repeat has been worked.

This method is applicable to many patterns and should be learnt and understood. The general principle is as follows: in turn, all pairs work through all the passives to make picots and work back through two pairs only. The last pair works back through the two passives, and on through sufficient pairs to make picots for the pattern. These picots are worked by taking the third pair from the edge and working out to the picot pin and back through the passives as far as the pattern. If the gimp thread is brought through each pair as it becomes available, there is less likelihood of mistakes being made.

Mayflower This occurs in different honeycomb fillings and consists of a cloth stitch diamond worked within the honeycomb. Before working the mayflower, the basic stitch arrangement must be fully understood. In order to work the mayflower the pins should be worked in the following order – referring to numbers on the previous head – 1, 2, 3, 4; 5, 6, 7; 8, 9; 14, 18. Pairs from 9 and 6 make a cloth stitch to begin the diamond, and the right hand pair becomes weaver and works from pin to pin as follows: 10, 11, 15, 12, 19, 16, 20 and 21. Pairs are taken in at 11, 15, 12 and 19; and left out after 12, 19, 20 and 16. Pin 21 is covered with a cloth stitch. All pairs leaving the cloth diamond are twisted twice each. The honeycomb is completed in the following order: 24, 25; 13, 22, 17, 23, 26; 27, 28, 29, 30.

Catch pins In Fig. 195 it can be seen that the ground stitches to the right of the head have been worked differently to earlier instructions. Whenever there are vertical rows of holes with ground one side of the gimp a catch pin may be used for neatness. The gimp passes through the pair from 4, is twisted three times, and works a ground stitch with the pair from e. Pin (7) is put up to the left of both pairs. Take the gimp through the left hand pair, twist it twice and work pin 7. The same method is used at pins (13) and (17).

The corner (Fig. 198) Complete the head immediately before the corner, also the sequence of picots to give three pairs for use in the corner head. Work the footside, and corner pin z. A new gimp is introduced through the pairs that would normally work the catch pin, instead they work honeycomb pin A inside the circle. Take the gimp through the next ground pair to the left and work honeycomb pin B. The left hand pair is released, and the gimp passes through it so that it is available for the next ring. Pass another new gimp through this pair and the next three pairs to the left (i.e. two from ground and one from honeycomb). The middle pairs work honeycomb pin C, and the right hand pairs work pin D. The right hand pair passes round both gimps to work pin E. Working pin F will complete the ring; enclose it with gimps, overlapping them below E and F. They are discarded. The left hand pairs inside the gimp work pin G, and from that pin the left hand pair goes to work the ground pins H and I. The right hand pair from G also leaves the ring to work pin J later. The honeycomb head must be worked completely before any further ground or honeycomb ring stitches can be made. At (c) make a false picot and work picot (d). At this stage the worker learns to assess the number of pairs required, and which pairs to use for the head.

It is obvious that the pair from G needs to work pin J, and the gimp will be taken to the right through all pairs including the pair from G. The seventh and eighth pairs to the left work pin a. Three pairs are required on the left to work honeycomb, and a false picot was made to provide the extra pairs. Pass the gimp through these three pairs. Work the honey-

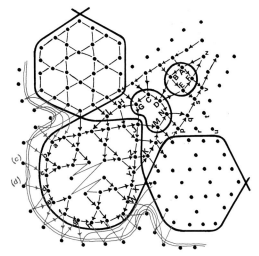

Fig. 198

comb continuous row to the right from a. Work gap row b. Work the first two pins in continuous row c, and pins d and e. Work the mayflower and complete the honeycomb, ending at pin j; enclose with gimp. Two pairs joined in at the false picot are no longer required and should be discarded in the passive pairs, as in the decorative strip. From the diagram, note that pairs from Z and Y work pin K. Pin L is worked before the ring can be completed. Pairs from L and J work pin M, and the ring is completed at N. Follow the diagram directional arrows to work the ground required for the next honeycomb head, remembering that the first continuous row of honeycomb must be worked before pin p.

LITTLE HEART

Requirements: Fourteen pairs of bobbins, Madeira Tanne no. 50. Refer to Figs 199 and 200. Prepare pricking 201.

Before starting to make the lace, study the diagram to understand the sequence of honeycomb holes. Frequently the holes are arranged to improve appearance rather than on a rigid grid.

To begin the pattern Select the longest row of ground holes and work as previously

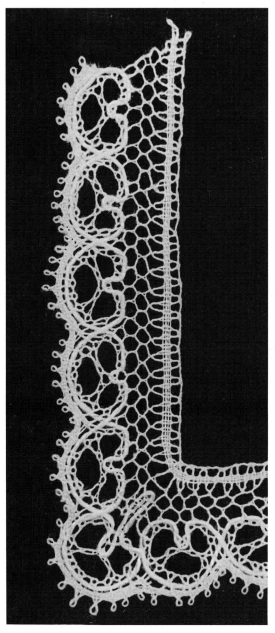

Fig. 199

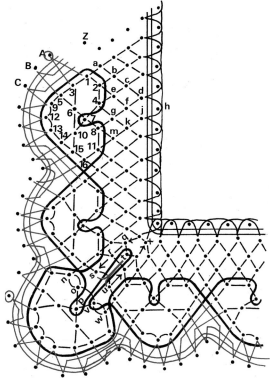

Fig. 200

explained to a. Continue until b, c and d are in position.

The headside This is an alternative method, introducing picots immediately. Make a false picot on pin A. Hang four pairs on support pin Z and take both pairs from A through these with cloth stitch. The third pair from the edge

works picot B and again the third pair works picot C. Remember to remove pin Z and ease the pairs into position.

Honeycomb Pass the gimp through pairs from C, B, A, a and b. Pairs from A and a work honeycomb pin 1, continue to pin 2. Take the right hand pair from 2 out round the gimp, twist three times and work ground pin e. Return round the gimp and twist twice. Work pins 3, 4 and ground pins f and, using the pair from 4, pin g. Work pins 5 and 6.

Nook pin Take the gimp through the pair from 4 and right side pair from 6 and twist each twice and work honeycomb pin 7. Take the gimp back through these pairs and the pair from g.

Work pin 8 and take the pair out ready for pin m. Now work the complete row of ground from h. Remember to work out to h with the fourth pair from the edge.

Complete the honeycomb in number order.

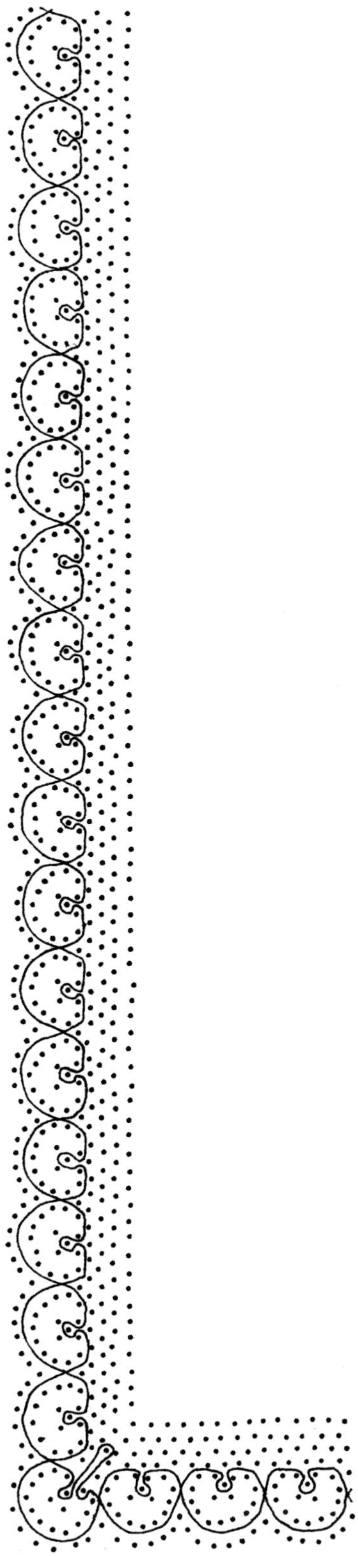

Fig. 201

Note that a pair goes out to make a picot from 9 and returns for 12. Similarly from 12 a pair makes a picot and returns for 13.

The picots from 13, 14, 15 and 16 are worked as in the Church Window pattern and provide four pairs for the next repeat.

The corner Follow the diagram. When honeycomb pin n has been covered, put up pin o between the pairs and cover with a honeycomb stitch. Work similarly at pins v and w. The gimp from p passes through two pairs from p, one pair from o, two from s and one from each of r and q. The left pair from s (indicated in blue) works cloth stitch through the three pairs. Pin t is put to the left of the weaver which works back through three pairs. The gimp is brought back through six pairs and pairs from o and p work nook pin v. Complete the honeycomb heart, discarding the two extra pairs. The original pairs from s (i.e. the weaver) and cloth passives work ground pin u. Work back to the corner with ground stitches, remember to place pin x to the right of both pairs. Use the corner pin twice. Continue.

RAM'S HORNS – WITH 'CUCUMBER' FOOT

Requirements: Eighteen pairs of bobbins, Madeira Tanne no. 50 and one gimp pair, Coton Perlé no. 8. An additional four pairs and one gimp pair are required for the corner. Refer to Figs 202 and 203. Prepare pricking 204.

Hang two pairs on A1, two pairs in order on B and C, and one pair on D, E, F and G.

To work cucumber foot The pairs on B and C are passive footside threads. Twist the pairs on A1 and cover with cloth stitch and three twists, work through the two passive pairs as usual and put up pin 2 to the right of the weaver. Twist the weaver twice and work back to footside pin 3 and to pin 4 with the pin to the right of the weaver. The weaver pair at D5 works through the two passive pairs from C and is

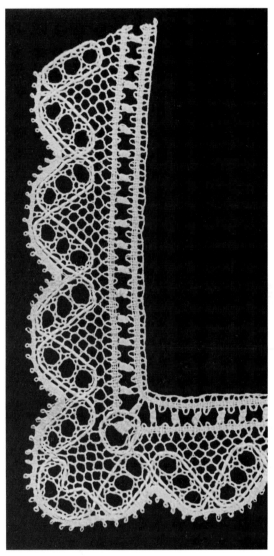

Fig. 202

twisted three times. Make a ground stitch with the pair from E and put catch pin 6 to the RIGHT of both pairs. Work ground pins 7 and 8 and remove support pins E, F and G. Take the pair immediately to the left of catch pin 6 and work to the right through the two passive pairs. Put up pin 9 to the left of the weaver. The pairs at 4 and 9 are twisted three times and work a tally. Refer to page 40. Twist threads each side three times each. The right side pair (including the tally weaver) work the footside later. The left pair works through two

pairs in cloth stitch, makes a ground stitch with the pair from 7. Pin 10 goes to the right of both pairs. Make ground stitch 11. Work back to pin 12 and on to catch pin 13. Remove support pins B and C. Fig. 205 shows that the footside is independent of the ground and is linked with tallies. The inner passives make a second footside which lacks the straight edge, this has the catch pins to the left and tallies to the right.

To work the honeycomb Hang up a gimp pair on G and pass it through six pairs hung on support pairs for the honeycomb. Pass the right gimp through pairs from 8 and 11. Hang two passive headside pairs on support pin H. Work in letter order from a to u. This includes ground stitch 1, picots at g, s and u and a honeycomb stitch at t. Cross the gimps below r and work seven rows of ground as far as pin 13. Work the next honeycomb feature from a to r with ground stitch g and picot 1.

The headside (ignore the additional thread at x unless working to the corner) The pairs from m, n, o, p and q work in order through the passive pairs, make a picot and return through two pairs only. When picot Q has been made, stop with the picot pair on the outside edge. Study the diagram and work a stitch at s in cloth stitch. Take the right pair from s round the gimp and leave it twisted ready for honeycomb pin a. The left pair is the inner passive. The picot pair at Q returns through six passive pairs, is twisted twice and passes round the gimp for pin b. Continue to make picots, each time using the third pair from the outer edge. Work two cloth stitches to the edge, make the picot and return through the remaining cloth pairs and round the gimp thread. One pattern repeat is complete.

The corner Hang two threads on a pin behind the work and let them become part of the cloth at position x. This is a simple way of adding an extra pair for use later. Work honeycomb area A and the headside picots to B. Work ground pins D, E and F. Work the ground as far as possible and complete the centre honeycomb

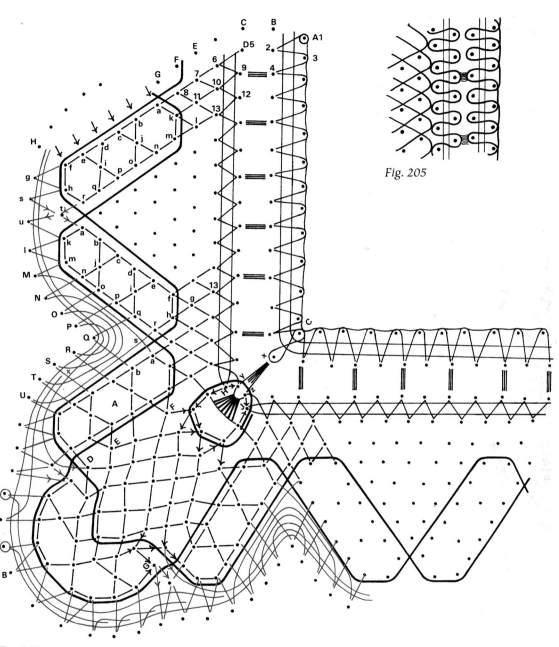

Fig. 205

Fig. 203

feature at G. Introduce a new gimp for the circle, beginning at pin H with the passive pairs making the honeycomb stitch. The corner weaver at x and the right pair from pin y make a tally. The tally weaver returns to the corner

pin C and the left pair works honeycomb pin z after the large tally within the circle has been made. The circle is completed at J. The additional five pairs on the headside are discarded in the cloth passive pairs.

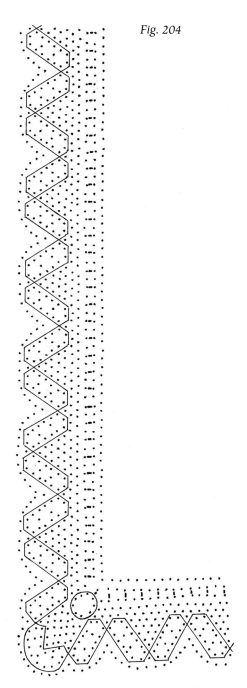

Fig. 204

The footside Begin at pins A and B and work cucumber foot as described in the previous pattern. Work three rows of ground to a, b and c.

The honeycomb ring Hang one gimp pair on C and two pairs on D. Pass the gimp through pairs from b, a and D. Twist pairs twice. Centre pairs work honeycomb stitch, pin d, honeycomb stitch. The left hand pairs work the honeycomb stitch, pin e, honeycomb stitch. Remove pins C and D and ease the pairs down. Replace pin D and hang on two passive headside pairs. Take the left pair from e, around the gimp, twist twice, and work two cloth stitches to the edge. Make a picot at f. Return with cloth stitch through two pairs, twist twice, pass round the gimp. Twist twice and work honeycomb pin g. Work honeycomb

PHEASANT'S EYE – WITH 'CUCUMBER' FOOT

Requirements: Eighteen pairs of bobbins, Madeira Tanne no. 50. One pair of gimp bobbins, Coton Perlé no. 8. Refer to Figs 206 and 207. Prepare pricking 208.

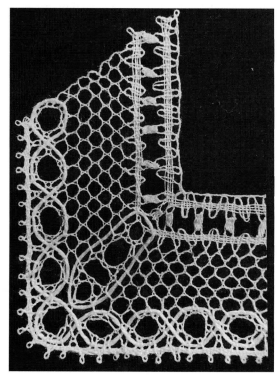

Fig. 206

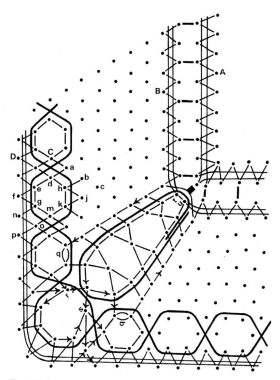

Fig. 207

pin h with pairs from d and b. The right pair
goes out to work ground pin j and returns for
honeycomb pin k. The right pair from g and
left pair from k work pin m. Cross the gimp
threads below m. The pair from g works picot
pin n and this pair and the pair from m work a
honeycomb pin at o. Work picot pin p and the
left side pairs are ready for the next ring. Work
three rows of ground and continue.

The corner At position q work honeycomb stitch,
pin, honeycomb stitch, pin, honeycomb stitch.
    The ring begins at r and ends at s. The
lozenge shape begins at t and ends at u.

PHEASANT'S EYE DECORATION

Requirements: Eighteen pairs of bobbins,
Madeira Tanne no. 50. Two pairs of gimp
bobbins, Coton Perlé no. 8. Refer to Figs
209 and 210. Prepare pricking 211.

This should be worked with reference to previous patterns as necessary. The picot at pin a is

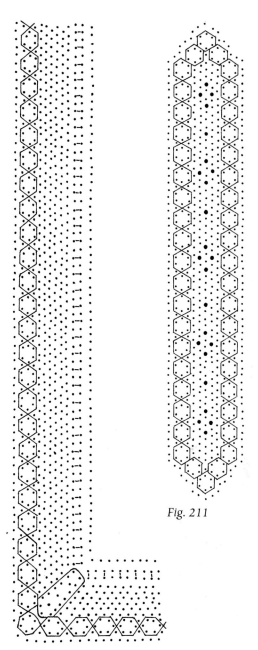

Fig. 211

Fig. 208

worked as follows: hang a pair on pin b. Pass
it round the gimp thread, twist it twice and
work out to make the picot at pin a. Remove
the support pin. This is not an ideal method as
the gimp may be distorted but it is acceptable
when one pair is needed to complete the picot
row. Add these holes to the pricking when
working the lace. Picot c is worked similarly.

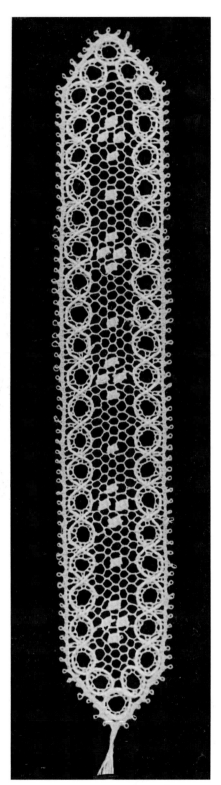

Fig. 209

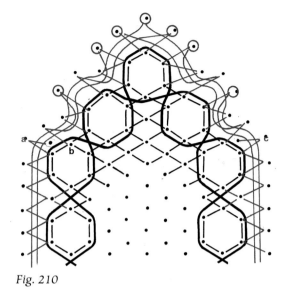

Fig. 210

THE KIDNEY BEAN PATTERN

Requirements: Seventeen pairs of bobbins, DMC Broder Machine no. 50, one pair gimp bobbins, Coton Perlé no. 8. Refer to Figs 212 and 213. Prepare pricking 214.

Work four rows of ground from A to a.

Prepare pairs for honeycomb as follows: hang three pairs on support pin C. Make false picot E and take the right pair through three pairs on support pin D. Work two more picots. Hang one pair on B. Pass the gimp thread through these pairs and twist the pairs twice. Two right side pairs from C work pin c. Continue to g, work picot h and return to j. Remember to remove support pins as soon as possible. The pair from B and the pair from ground row A work pin m, continue to o and ground stitch p. Work honeycomb, in letter order, in preparation for the gimp feature. Take the gimp through as shown and work the central ring with the tally. Complete the honeycomb and continue. The corner is straightforward, no additional pairs are necessary.

Fig. 212

Fig. 213

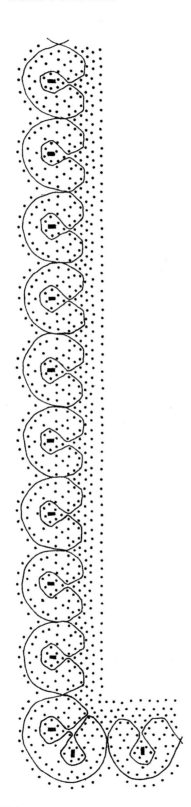

CLOTH AND HONEYCOMB FAN PATTERN

Requirements: Nineteen pairs of bobbins, DMC Broder Machine 50. One pair gimp bobbins coton Perlé no. 8. Refer to Figs 215 and 216. Prepare pricking 217.

Begin at A and work seven rows of ground to a. Hang pairs on a support pin for the honeycomb and then work the picot head as indicated. Pass the gimp through seven pairs on each side and work honeycomb pins b to j. Work the cloth diamond with the six pin hole. Complete the honeycomb from k to v. Cross the gimp threads below v. Work the picots and ground in preparation for the next fan.

To work the corner Follow the diagram, no additional pairs are required, but only one passive remains at the outer edge.

Fig. 214

Fig. 215

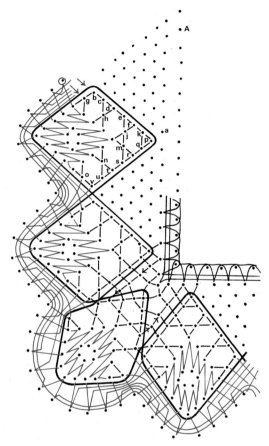

Fig. 216

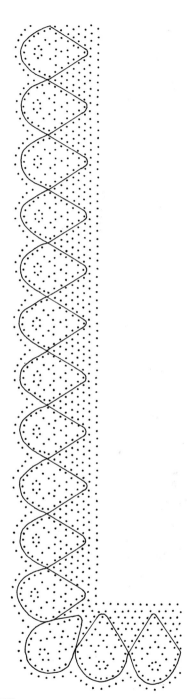

Fig. 217

PATTERN INTERPRETATION

Refer to Fig. 218. Without photograph and working diagram, the lacemaker has to interpret the pricking. There are several possibilities:

A This area can be (a) ground with tallies (b) honeycomb – but two complete rows of honeycomb close together is unattractive (c) honeycomb with diagonal cloth either side of the diamonds.

B The diamonds can be worked as (a) open honeycomb rings (b) honeycomb rings with tallies or (iii) cloth stitch diamonds.

C Ground worked with or without tallies.

Choice should be made to achieve a balanced effect.

To work the pattern

Requirements: Twenty-three pairs of bobbins, DMC Broder Machine no. 50. One pair and one single gimp bobbin, Coton Perlé no. 8. Six extra pairs and two gimp pairs are required for the corner. Refer to Figs 219 and 220. Prepare pricking 221.

Work ten rows of ground. Introduce the gimp threads as shown in the diagram. Work honeycomb from a to the headside, then from b. Work the cloth stitch trail from c to d. At the same time work the picot edge as necessary. Work the honeycomb diamond in order, using the same gimp thread for f and g. Work the cloth from d to j and then honeycomb from k to l and from m to n.

The corner Before the rings A, B and C are worked begin the cloth feature O. To join in two pairs, one for the cloth and the other for the ground, work as follows:- place two pairs round a pin at p. Pass the gimp thread through the right side threads and begin the cloth at o. Remove pin p and twist the threads three times, these are the right side pairs for the ground stitch at p.

Work the honeycomb rings A, B and C. The gimp passes through the pairs which make the bottom stitch in each ring. When the pin has been covered the gimp travels to the left for the next ring.

When A, B and C are complete, turn the pillow diagonally. Unfortunately the three cloth features must be worked at the same time as pairs pass from one to the next. Pairs are joined in at u and v as at o. When the cloth is complete, turn the pillow again to continue the lace.

Note that the six extra pairs – marked by blue arrows – when no longer required travel with gimp threads until they are securely fastened into the work, they are then discarded.

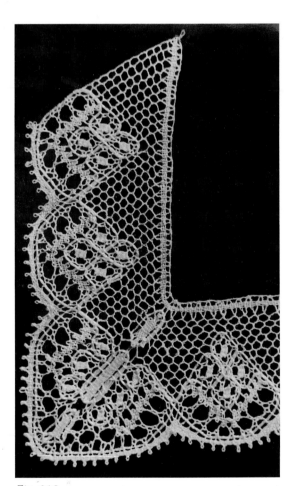

Fig. 219

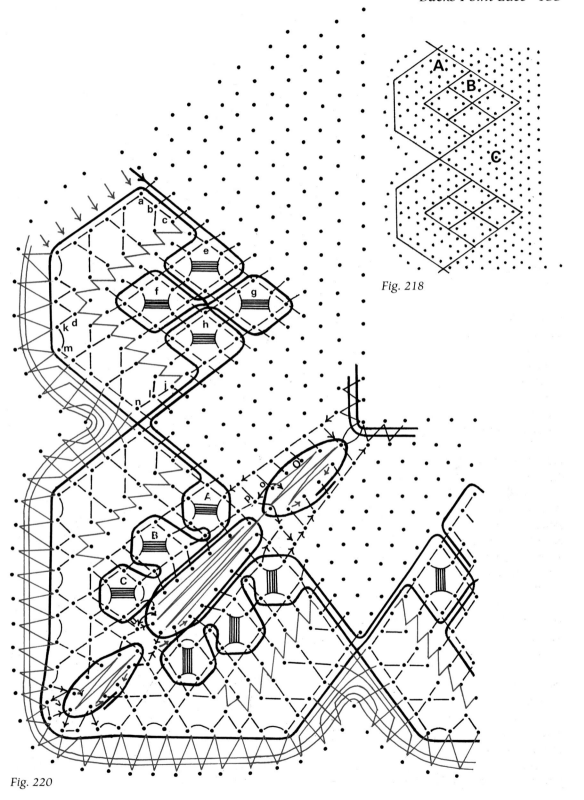

Fig. 218

Fig. 220

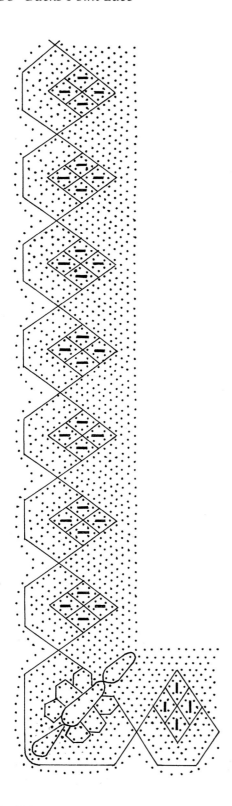

BLACK LACE WITH KAT STITCH GROUND

Requirements: Twenty-six pairs of bobbins, Madeira Tanne no. 80. Two pairs of gimp bobbins, Coton Perlé no. 8 or no. 12. Refer to Figs 222 and 223. Prepare pricking 224.

Honeycomb rings and half stitch are always found in Kat stitch patterns which are traditionally worked in black thread.

Kat stitch ground Hang three pairs round A1 and two pairs on B, C, D, E and F inclusive. Twist the two right hand bobbins three times and work cloth stitch through the other two pairs on A1. Continue with this pair, which is third from the right edge, through the next two pairs from B in cloth stitch and twist. Put up pin 2 to the right of the weaver (i.e. between the last pairs worked, but do not cover the pin. Use the weaver to work in cloth stitch and twist through two more pairs (from C) and put up pin 3 to the right of the weaver. Remove support pin B and others as necessary. Continue, work through two pairs and put up the pin, until 4, 5 and 6 are in position.

Working from left to right and *without* pins, cross the pairs *between* the pins with cloth stitch and twist. To the right of pin, 2, there are three pairs and one edge pair; work cloth stitch and twist with the two nearest to pin 2. The footside pin is worked using the third pair from the edge. Work cloth stitch and twist through two pairs, put pin 7 inside two pairs as usual, twist the outer pair once more and discard to the side of the pillow. Cover the pin. To continue Kat stitch take the third pair from the edge, work cloth stitch and twist through the next two pairs to the left, put pin 8 to the right of the weaver. Work pins 9, 10 and 11. Work rows from 12 to 15 and 17 to 19. Study the lace and understand that pins support the pairs travelling diagonally.

Fig. 221

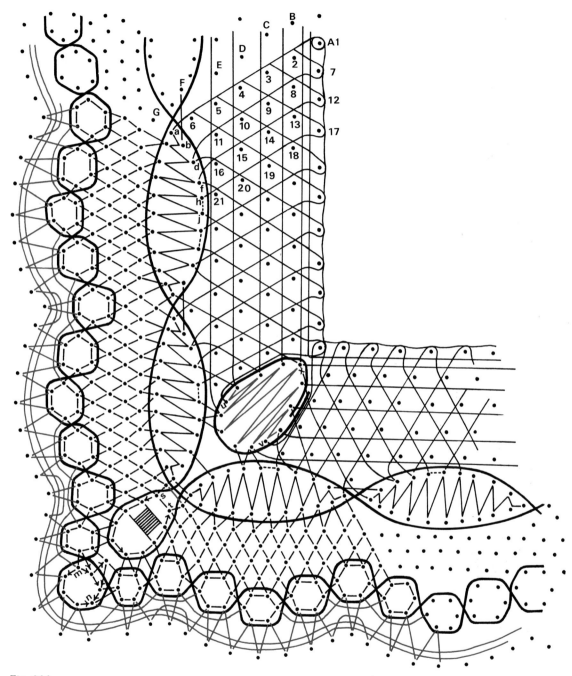

Fig. 223

The head, point ground and honeycomb rings
Work as shown in the diagram. Half stitch
feature. The diagram shows the use of ground
pairs on the left, only the right side will be
explained. The difficulty is to marry together

Kat stitch and the pattern features. Always
ensure that the diagonal is continuous from
the foot pins and that the vertical pairs are
very straight.

Hang one pair on F and one on G. The

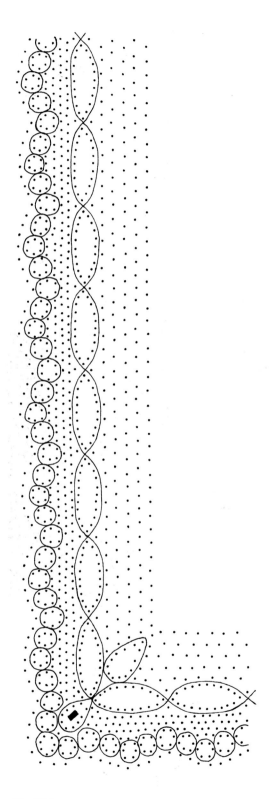

Fig. 224

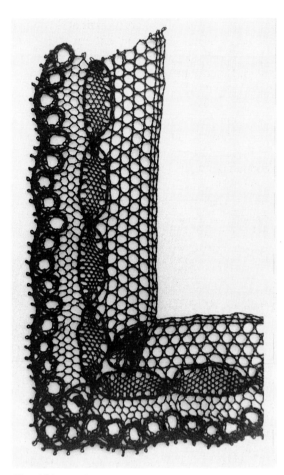

Fig. 222

travelling pair to the left of pin 6 works through the vertical pair from F to pass round a gimp to begin the half stitch with the pair from support pin G. Therefore there are always three pairs at the beginning and end of the half stitch. This is necessary to provide sufficient pairs for the half stitch feature. The vertical pair is brought in at b. The travelling pair to the left of 11 passes through a vertical pair to enter the half stitch at d. It is left out after the pin and passes back through the same vertical pair. The travelling pair to the left of 15 works cloth stitch and twist stitch through two pairs and pin 16 is put in position. It continues through the vertical pair to enter half stitch at f. Again it is left out and passes back through the vertical pair. Cross the pairs between 15 and 16 (no pin) and work 20 and 21. The travelling pair from

21 passes through the vertical pair and enters the half stitch at h but is not left out until pin j is covered. Continue to work ground and half stitch. If necessary mark the pairs of bobbins hanging vertically.

The corner There are no additional pairs required. Begin the ring with the tally at s and finish at t. The travelling pair from the corner footside pin works the ground row without pins to enter the half stitch at u. It is left out at v and travels back to the corner without pins. Notice that two pairs are brought in for pin x and left out immediately. The headside honeycomb ring begins at pin m and ends at pin n.

Circular Patterns

The attractive old circular patterns are usually most elaborate, but for the experienced worker with plenty of time they are well worthwhile. Simple motifs useful for small doilies, for decoration and for mounting under glass under paperweights or trays are quick to make and require only a basic knowledge of Bucks point lace. They require comparatively few bobbins and are easy to design.

The patterns consist of six triangular heads around a centre point. An understanding of the method of designing will facilitate the working. Refer to the first motif, Fig. 225 and the Sheep's Head pattern on page 114. The lace is worked at an angle of 60 degrees from the footside. If six heads are placed about a centre point a small motif results. Begin by marking a six pin honeycomb ring on to a grid at 60 degrees. Divide the sheet into sections by joining opposite points of the ring through the centre and extending the lines outside the centre ring. The stitches on these lines fall between sections and can be honeycomb or ground. The pattern is placed within each section, and the picots arranged as necessary.

SHEEP'S HEAD

Requirements: Ten pairs of bobbins, Madeira Tanne no. 50. One pair and one single gimp bobbin, Coton Perlé no. 8. Refer to Figs 225 and 226. Prepare pricking 227.

Mark the position XX on the pillow with a braid or extra cover cloth. This is the same position as the footside on a straight edging.

Make a false picot at A and work the right pair through two passive pairs from a support pin. Work a normal picot at b. Pass a gimp pair through these pairs and five pairs from a support pin. Work the honeycomb head completely, cross the gimps and take them on through pairs from u and v. Work pin w in honeycomb and cross the gimps below the pin.

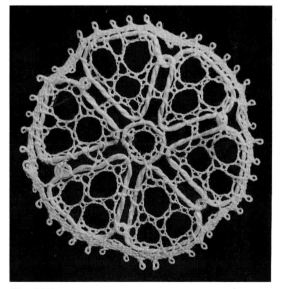

Fig. 225

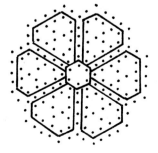

Fig. 227

Pairs from s and t work honeycomb pin x. The pair from r and a pair from a support pin pass round the single gimp to honeycomb pin y. On the headside the pair from picot d travels back through the passives and round pin z and back for picot a.

Turn the pillow so that the footside equivalent is indicated YY. Work the next head and then move the markers to ZZ.

It will be necessary to push the pins from the earlier sections down into the pillow so that the last two sections can be worked. A piece of clear plastic film placed over the pin heads and held in position by cover cloths will make the working easier.

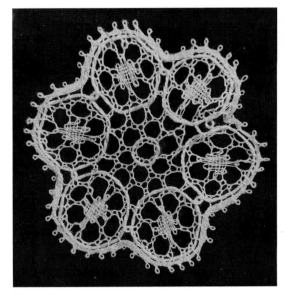

Fig. 228

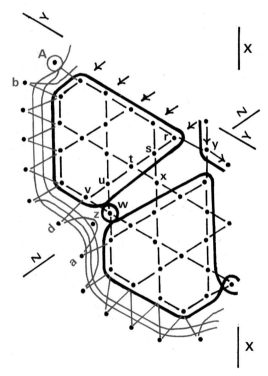

Fig. 226

CHURCH WINDOW

Requirements: Fourteen pairs of bobbins, DMC Broder Machine no. 50. One pair and one single gimp bobbins, Coton Perlé no. 8. Refer to Figs 228 and 229. Prepare pricking 230.

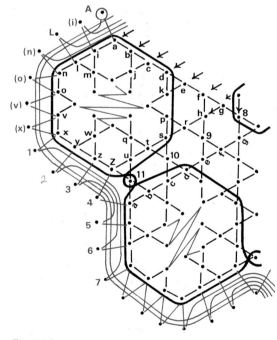

Fig. 229

The Church Window pattern has been adapted, and honeycomb stitches used instead of ground. The gap row falls on the line between sections. This is advantageous as no pair leads into the centre, and therefore no

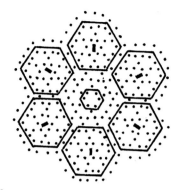

Fig. 230

pair is discarded. The general method is the same as for the previous pattern.

Hang up four pairs for use in the heading. Make a false picot at A and picots at (i), L and (n). Pass the gimp through the four pairs from the picots, and through four pairs hung up on the right for use in the honeycomb head. Hang up three more pairs behind for use at e, f and g. Work in letter order the pins from a to z and Z. After pin o, work a mayflower. Enclose the head with gimps, and cross them below u. Work picot pins 1 to 7 inclusive. Hang up a single gimp and an ordinary pair to the left of it behind pin 8. Pass the gimp through this pair, and the pair from g, and work honeycomb pin 8. Take the gimp back through the left hand pair. Work gap row pins 9 and 10.

Take the right hand gimp through the pair from u, and the left hand gimp through the pair from Z. Work honeycomb pin 11 and enclose with gimp. Take the gimp through the pairs for the next section. Move the extra cover cloth to the next position.

CIRCULAR MAT

Refer to Figs 231 and 232. Prepare pricking 233.

This is designed and worked in the same way as the small motifs, between each section is a row of honeycomb stitches. Three different fillings are shown but the worker may select one for all sections if preferred, refer to Figs 234a, 234b, 234c.

To begin Place an extra cover cloth to the side of the section to be worked and parallel to the

line YY. XX indicates the honeycomb stitches. The first ring to be worked in each section is marked on the pricking with a broken vertical line, this also indicates top and bottom holes. A false picot is made at A and the right side pair passes through nine pairs from a support pin. Work picot B normally using the third pair from the edge. Hang one pair on a and two on the other honeycomb pins on XX. Pass a gimp through the pairs from B, A, a and b to work ring 1. Outside the gimp, on the left picot C is made and on the right a honeycomb stitch with the other pair from b at c. *Remember to remove support pins as soon as the stitches have been worked.* The gimp remains either side and a new gimp passes through a pair from D, the inner passive pair, the pairs from y, x, c and d. Work ring 2 and continue to the cloth stitch feature. Return to ring 8 and work the filling and the rings around the edge. It is not possible to complete ring 16 until the centre has been worked.

Refer to Fig. 235 and ascertain that the long row of honeycomb has been worked to p. Take the gimp through the necessary pairs and work the entire cloth stitch feature. The pair brought in at r, is left out after t.

Another gimp is required for the centre ring. The pair from s and a pair from a support pin work honeycomb pin u, the right hand pair remains within the gimp ring throughout.

Complete the section at pin h in ring 17. From the centre honeycomb j on XX work the stitches independently to k. Both gimps cross above and below k. Turn the pillow and continue. Joining is explained on page 176.

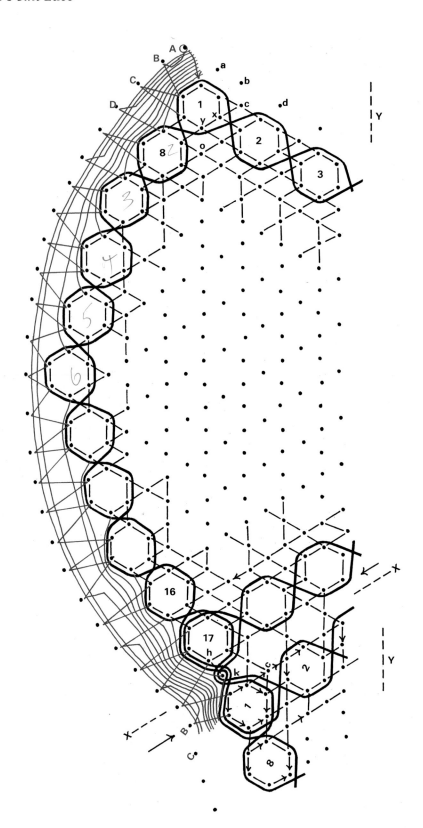

Fig. 232

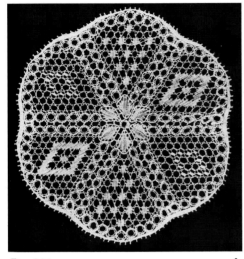

Fig. 231

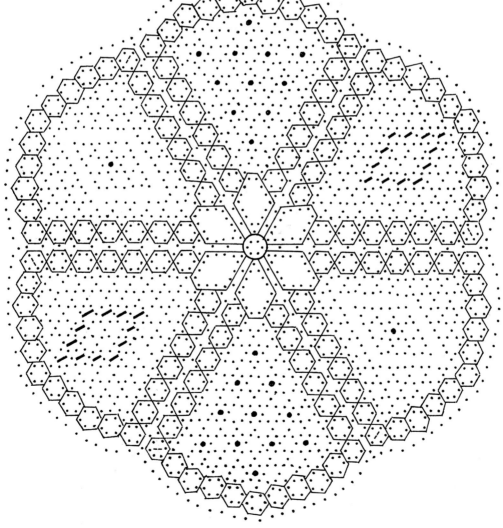

Fig. 233

Fig. 234a

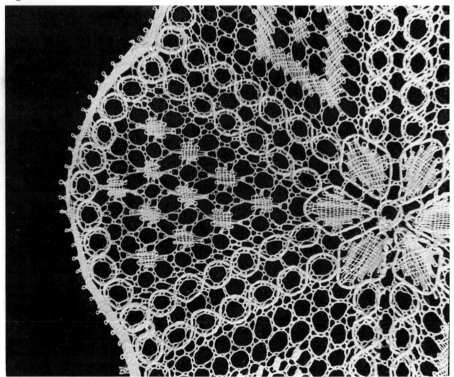

Fig. 234b

Fig. 234c

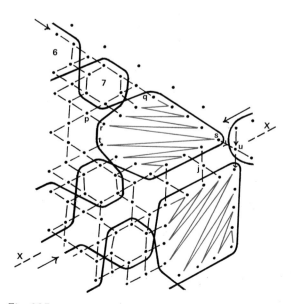

Fig. 235

Principles of Bucks Point Design

Workers who wish to enjoy the more advanced old patterns, or who wish to adapt or design Bucks Point lace, require a good basic knowledge of practical lace making, and an understanding of the way in which patterns are made. Many patterns, particularly the narrow edgings are quite geometric in design, but many have the beauty of flowers and scrolls which run freely through the lace. However, all Bucks Point patterns have a geometric basis. The angle between the footside and the diagonal row of ground is somewhere between 52 and 70 degrees. Refer to Fig. 180 on page 111. Usually all the stitches with the exception of cloth are worked at the same angle. Occasionally, there may be a slight variation in the honeycomb in an old pattern.

The appearance of the lace depends to a large extent on the choice of angle. Many narrow edgings are worked at an angle of 52 to 55 degrees, whereas the wide, elaborate patterns are usually worked at 60 to 70 degrees. In lace made at the angle of 70 degrees, the cloth work will be very close; but it will be more even at 55 degrees. Refer to Fig. 236. Notice also, the change in the shape of the four pin buds, the sharp pointed buds are unattractive unless the lace is very fine. The coarser the lace and thread, the more obvious any defects become.

On page 183 there is a selection of grids and ground dots. Often it is helpful to plot a pattern very much enlarged, similar to the diagrams in this book.

Ground (Fig. 237) The holes are spaced evenly at the required angle. Note the position, the distance between catch pin and footside is greater than elsewhere to provide space for the two passive pairs. It is good practice to add the footside row of holes first. Place a lace pin in the holes at both ends of the line. Push a straight edge against the pins and prick the straight line.

Tallies occur in ground and are worked instead of the stitch. When pricking, mark the position with a large ink dot. Method of working is explained on page 119.

Gimp Fingers in ground (Fig. 237) The best advice is to move the gimp to the positions indicated, work in letter order, and pass the gimp through when necessary. There are twists both sides of the gimp, either added or part of the preceding stitch. There are no twists between gimps which lie together. Ground stitches are used throughout.

Cucumber foot (Fig. 238) This is a variation and is pricked as shown. The black dots indicate the grid and the blue rings indicate the pricking of ground and cucumber foot. The second and third rows of holes must be exactly opposite each other for the tallies. The method of working is explained on page 125.

Kat stitch This is rarely found in white lace, but frequently in black. It is usual to use a 60° grid and the holes are further apart than for Bucks Point ground. This varies but the use of 12/25 mm (12/1 in) grid for the Bucks Point ground and 8/25 mm (8/1 in) grid for the kat stitch within the same pattern is recommended. Method of working is explained on page 136.

Honeycomb (Fig. 239) This is plotted over ground holes. The method of working is explained on page 116. When patterns are not geometric it is more difficult to find the diagonal lines on which to base the working. Look for diamond shapes with the obtuse angle at the top. Honeycomb was called 'fivepin' and this referred to the five pins in the X indicated in the diagram.

Variations:

1   The cloth stitch diamond known as 'Mayflower' is explained on page 122.
2   The cloth stitch diamond known as 'Old Mayflower' – the diamond is worked in letter order. At d and e no pairs enter the diamond and the weaver is given extra twists. Nothing is left out after h and i, and the weaver is given extra twists again.

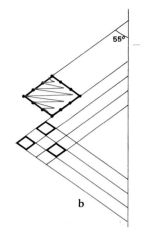

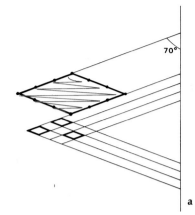

Fig. 236

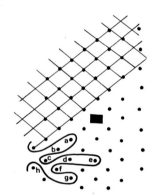

Fig. 237

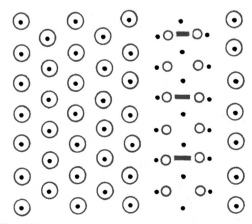

Fig. 238

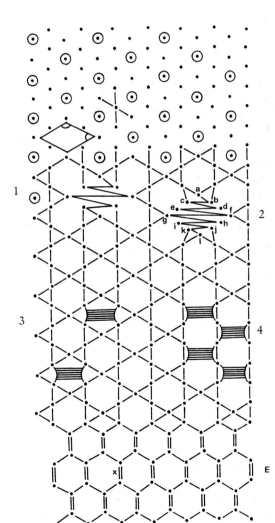

Fig. 239

3 Tallies worked within the honeycomb is explained on page 147.
4 Tallies worked in place of honeycomb holes – the pairs which normally make the honeycomb stitch work a tally instead.
5 There are a number of old fillings which are worked in honeycomb stitch although the hole arrangement is different. At position x, work honeycomb stitch, pin, honeycomb stitch, pin, honeycomb stitch. This is known as pin chain.

6 Vertical cloth trails and tallies (Fig. 240) The diagram indicates the method of making a pricking. The weavers work through two pairs to form vertical strips of cloth or half stitch and the weavers from each strip meet and work a tally at the intervals indicated on the pricking. This is similar to cucumber foot.
7 Pin chain and tallies (Fig. 241) Every hole is worked in honeycomb stitch, pin, honeycomb stitch as follows. Work pins a and b. Take the inner pairs, make a tally, and then work pins c and d. The right hand pair from d with a left hand pair from e make a tally to g and h. Similarly, the left hand pair from c and the right hand pair from f makes a tally to j and k. The inner pairs at k and g work a tally, and so on. Sometimes the tallies are not as close together as illustrated lower, in the diagram.

Nook Pins The nook pin anchors the gimp thread closely in the cloth feature in the pattern. Fig. 242 indicates the use of the weaver and the lack of twists adjacent to the cloth stitch. Fig. 243 illustrates three positions of the nook pin.

a The weaver remains the same throughout.
b The weaver completes the right side and loses its function as weaver. The gimp is brought round to the nook pin and through the first free passive pair. The nook pin is put up, the gimp brought back and the passive becomes the new weaver.

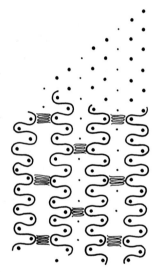

Fig. 240

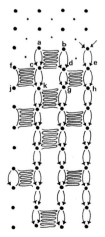

Fig. 241

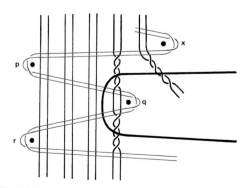

Fig. 242

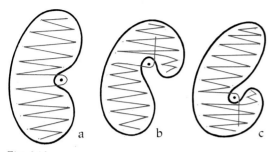

Fig. 243

c The weaver passes out round the gimp, the nook pin is put in and the weaver becomes a passive pair. The gimp taken upwards to accept pairs for the cloth. The cloth is restarted and a new weaver completes the feature.

DECORATIVE SAMPLER WITH FIVE DIFFERENT FILLINGS

Requirements: Thirty-six pairs of bobbins, DMC Broder Machine no. 50. Two pairs of gimp bobbins, Coton Perlé no. 8. Refer to Figs 244 and 245a. Prepare pricking 246. In the fifth filling, the short lines should be pricked as holes to make diamonds with four holes on each side.

To begin Make false picots at A and B. Hang four pairs round a pin at position X. Hang one gimp pair to fall with the threads together in the centre. Work the right pair from A in cloth stitch through the four threads from X. Twist and pass round the gimp thread. Repeat similarly with the left pair from B. Work honeycomb pin a. Continue the headside referring back to page 119 if necessary.

The second gimp is put in as described on page 141. Fig. 245b shows the method of arranging the gimp threads between fillings. *Filling 1.* (Fig. 247a) Mayflower in honeycomb, refer to page 122.

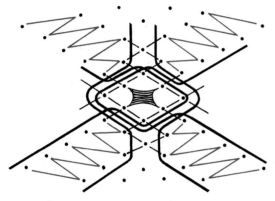

Fig. 245b

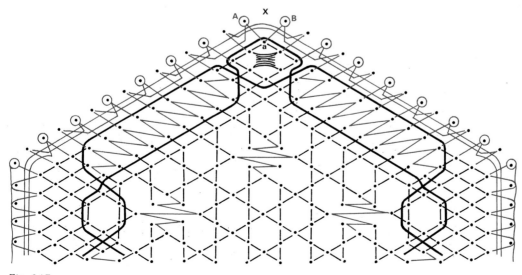

Fig. 245a

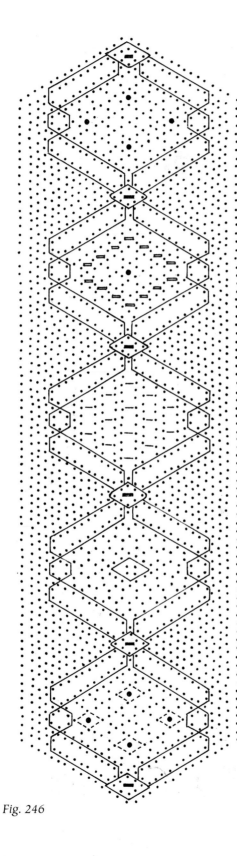

Fig. 246

Fig. 244

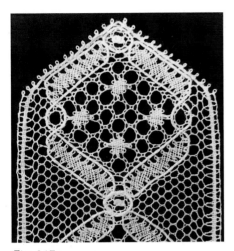

Fig. 247a

Fig. 247c

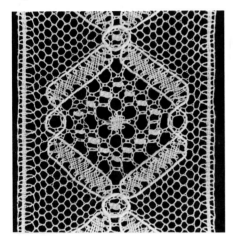

Fig. 247b

Fig. 247d

Filling 2. (Fig. 247b) Tallies within honeycomb rings and central mayflower, refer to page 147.
Filling 3. (Fig. 247c) Vertical cloth bars and tallies, refer to page 240.
Filling 4. (Fig. 247d) Hexagonal honeycomb with a cloth diamond. Refer to Fig. 284e for the filling and page 103 for the hole in the cloth diamond.
Filling 5. (Fig. 247e) Old mayflower. Refer to page 146.

To complete the work refer to page 120.

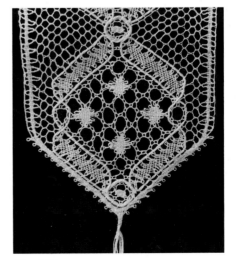

Fig. 247e

Corners

Apart from the truly beautiful wedding hand-kerchiefs, corners are seldom found in Bucks Point lace.

The Torchon corner is easy to work as the pillow is turned through 90° and the lace continued on the next side. As Bucks Point lace is worked at a different angle this is not possible and a new feature must be introduced to separate the rows of ground which would otherwise converge and be unworkable.

A corner may be achieved as follows:

1 Extending a honeycomb shape from head to foot, refer to page 157.
2. Arranging the existing pattern feature across the corner, refer to page 123. This is the most popular method.

3 Creating a new feature which harmonizes with the design.

Notice that 2 and 3 require additions to break the ground area. For example:

(a) the addition of small rings across the ground area, refer to page 123.
(b) the addition of cloth or half stitch features, refer to pages 134 and 138.
(c) the use of gimp thread, refer to page 124.
(d) the use of a combination of the above.

To make the pricking (Figs 248a and 248b):

1 Make several photocopies of the edging pricking.
2 Cut the pricking to leave a complete pattern repeat plus two footside holes.
3 Cut a second pricking to provide the mirror image. Alternatively the first piece is pricked and turned over (the rough side is now on top).
4 Mark in the diagonal line at 45°.
5 Over a sheet of plain paper, place the prickings together (Fig. 248b).
6 Cut a pattern feature and mark in the centre line.

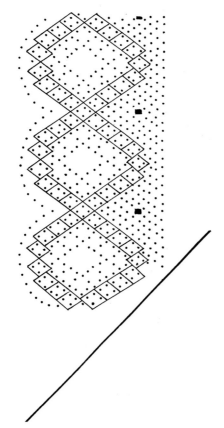

Fig. 248a

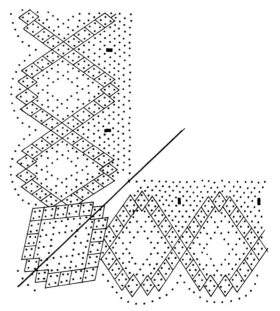

Fig. 248b

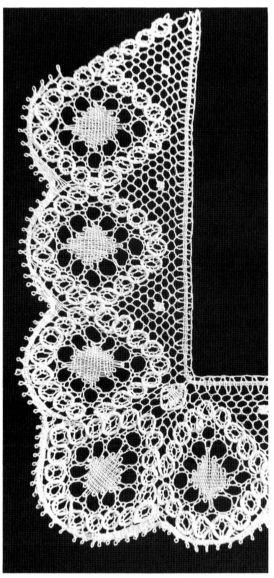

Fig. 249

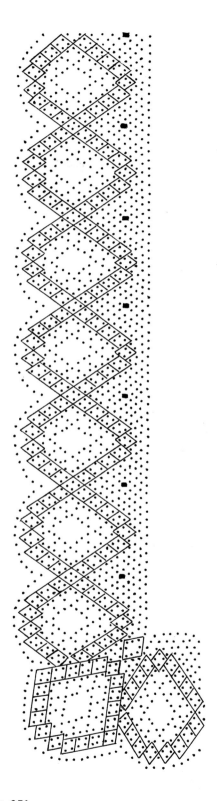

Fig. 251

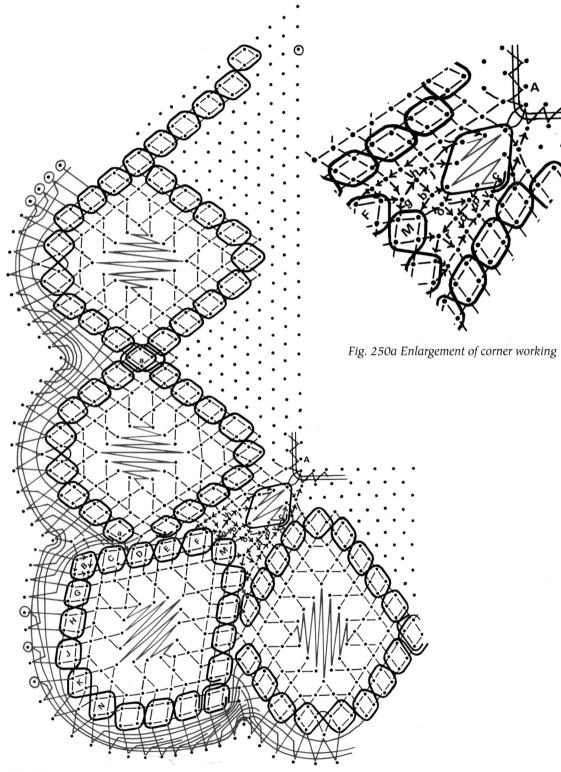

Fig. 250a Enlargement of corner working

Fig. 250

7   Place in position, using the 45° line as a guide. There is no problem in this pattern but the feature must extend outwards to provide a well rounded – not flat – corner.

8   Use a ruler to draw lines parallel with the footside and diagonally to position the ground holes. Add the diamond 'by eye' ascertaining that the points are on the 45° line. It is necessary to add the ground holes at this stage as space is limited and they lie closer together than in the original pricking.

9   Work out the arrangement of picot holes.

10   Prick the pattern.

CLOTH STITCH DIAMOND WITH FOUR PIN BUDS PATTERN

Requirements: Twenty-six pairs of bobbins, DMC Broder Machine no. 50, two pairs of gimp bobbins, Coton Perlé no. 8. Extra bobbins are needed for the corner.

Refer to Figs 249 and 250. Prepare pricking 251.

The corner Work the ground row from A. Turn the pillow diagonally. Work the four pin buds from B to F. *At the completion of the honeycomb ring at pin a the spare pair is carried with the gimp towards the ground and will later work pin b.* Work ground pins g and h. The pair with the gimp from a works ground pin b with the pair from h. Work the cloth stitch diamond. One spare pair from c is carried with the gimp and discarded.

Work buds G, H and J, introducing false picots as indicated. Begin the honeycomb and work buds K and M. Complete the necessary honeycomb stitches to work the central cloth diamond. Work bud N and complete the honeycomb. Make ground stitches o, p, q and r and complete the buds. Remember to discard pairs in the headside passives. The pair from c works pin v and is discarded with the gimp. Turn the pillow and continue.

Decorative handkerchief corners

Requirements: Pairs of bobbins as required, DMC Broder Machine no. 50 and Coton Perlé no. 8.

THE HEART DESIGN

Refer to Fig. 252. Prepare pricking 253.

This is geometric and the easiest of the three corners, detailed Fig. 254 clarifies the working of the centre cloth and honeycomb with tallies.

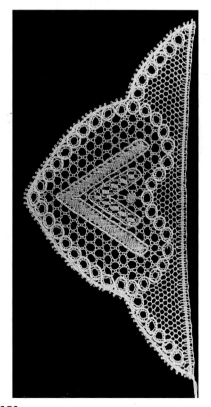

Fig. 252

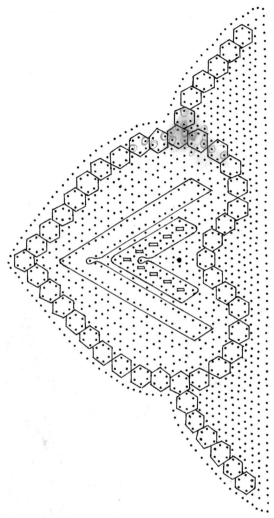

Fig. 253

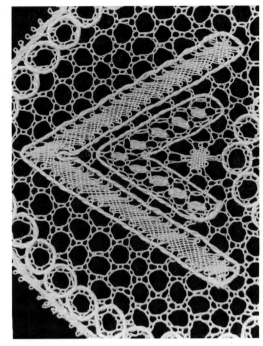

Fig. 254

Fig. 257

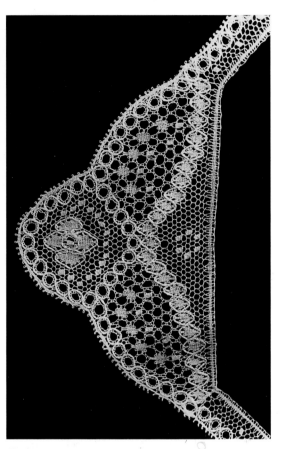

Fig. 255

THE GARLAND DESIGN

Refer to Fig. 255. Prepare pricking 256.

This can be worked without the handkerchief edging, starting with a honeycomb ring,
a, and cloth diamond, b. Refer also to detailed
Fig. 257.

A narrow edging adds to the attractive
appearance of a handkerchief, the edging Fig.
258 is quick to make. Cut the pattern (Fig.
259) to size and make the pricking. Working is
similar to the lace on page 128.

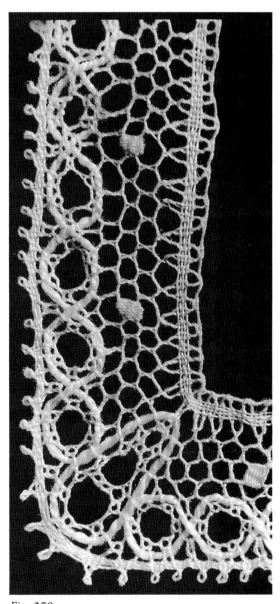

Fig. 258

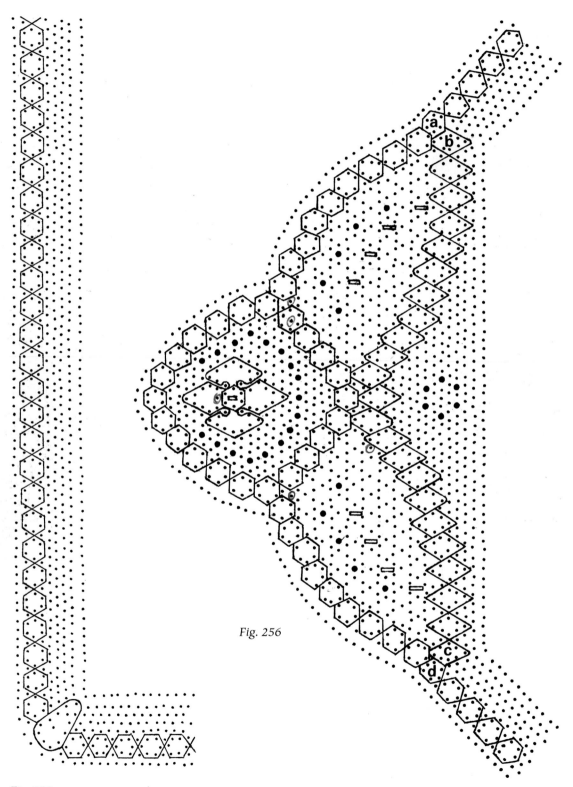

Fig. 256

Fig. 259

FLORAL CORNER

Refer to Fig. 260. Prepare pricking 261, the
edging on page 129 will match this pattern,
if reduced to 90% of the orginal.
Fig. 262 explains the working of the floral
feature.

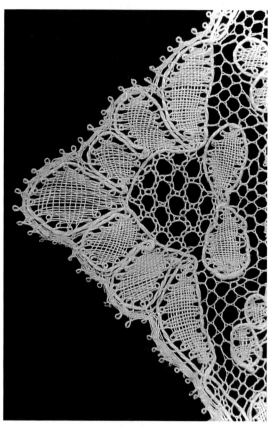

Fig. 262

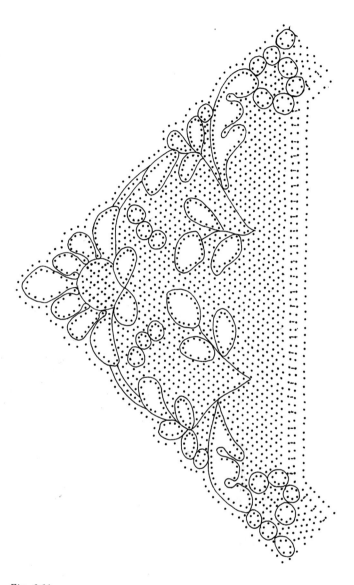

Fig. 261

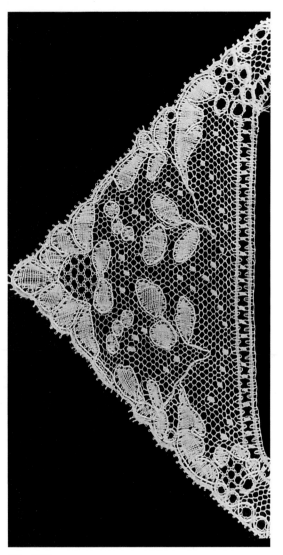

Fig. 260

Fine Bucks patterns

Old lace was made with very fine thread, using thin pins on a pricking with the holes very close together. Many narrow edgings are delightful worked in this way, but lose their beauty when enlarged. Today, with the modern photocopier, patterns can be enlarged or reduced quickly. The last twelve patterns look more attractive when worked on a pricking with thirteen or more holes to 1 inch (25 mm) on the footside. Madeira Tanne no. 80 is a suitable thread used with Coton Perlé no. 8 or no. 12.

To satisfy present-day needs corners have been prepared for some patterns, the corners for these patterns are very straightforward to work and require no additional pairs. However, corners contrived for wide geometric edgings are rarely successful.

PATTERN 1

Figs 263, 264 and 265. A pattern that is very
quick to work. The headside picots are worked
in the same way as Sheep's Head on page 000.

The corner Work the corner pin A and the
catch pin. Place a gimp thread through the

Fig. 263

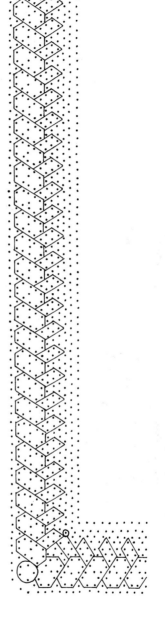

Fig. 265

pairs for ground pin B. The gimp encloses the
pin and is discarded. Complete the cloth C and
honeycomb D. Work the corner ring E from a
to b. Turn the pillow and continue the next
side.

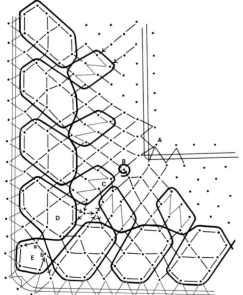

Fig. 264

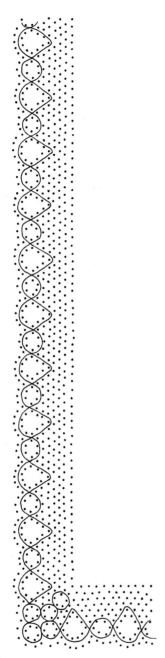

Fig. 267

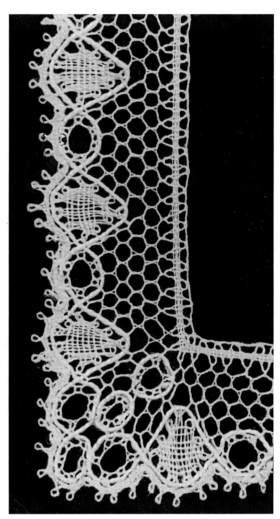

Fig. 266

PATTERN 2

Figs 266, 267 and 268. *The corner* Work ring A pins a and b and c1. Work ring B pins c and d. Complete ring C. Work ring D, beginning at e and finishing at f. Turn the pillow and begin ring E. Complete ring B at g. complete ring A at h.

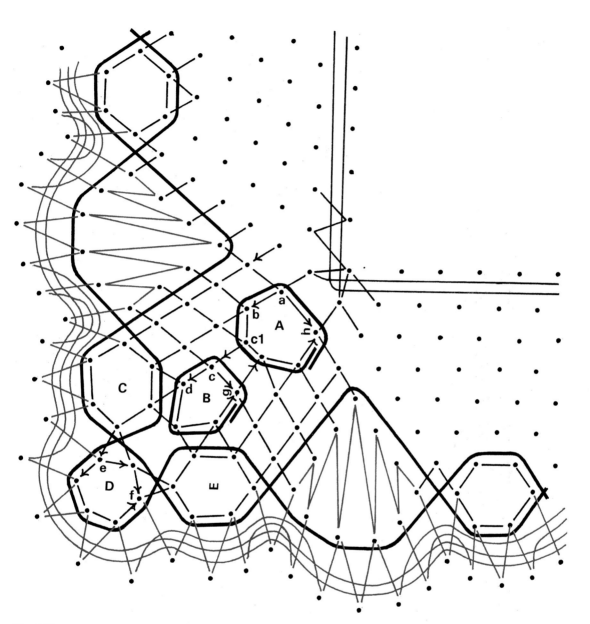

Fig. 268

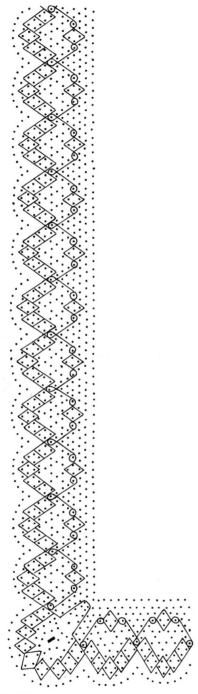

Fig. 271

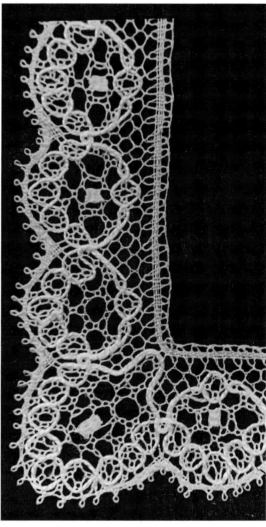

Fig. 269

PATTERN 3

Figs 269, 270 and 271. Two gimp pairs are required. In the diagram the right side pair has been indicated with a thinner line to clarify its movement. However, the same thickness Coton Perlé is used for both. Begin the corner honeycomb at a and complete it at b.

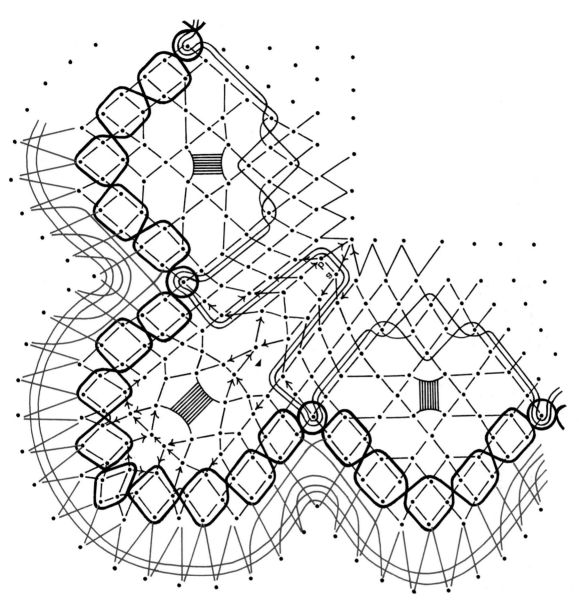

Fig. 270

PATTERN 4

Figs 272, 273 and 274. Complete the cloth stitch feature by working from a to b through three pairs, cover pin b. The pair left out at a enters the ground and the left hand pair from b goes out to make a picot. The centre pair travels through the gimp and works the top honeycomb pin c with the other pair from b.

Fig. 272

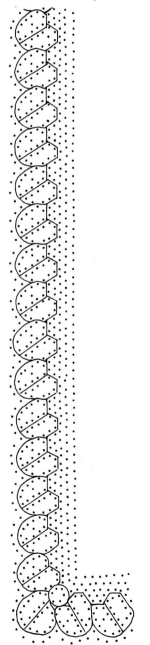

Fig. 274

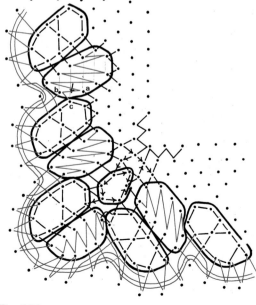

Fig. 273

PATTERN 5

Figs 275, 276 and 277. Pin a is a nook pin at
the base of the cloth diamond. Before working
the last pin take the gimp through both pairs,
i.e. the passive and weaver pairs. Work the
pin, cloth stitch, pin a, cloth stitch. Take the
gimp back through both pairs and continue
through the pairs required for the next cloth
diamond.

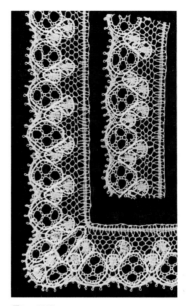

Fig. 275

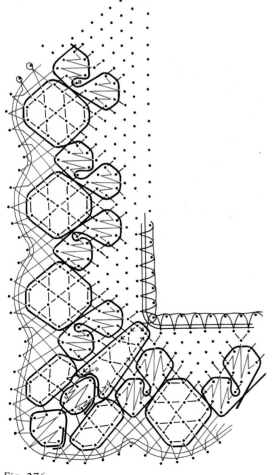

Fig. 276

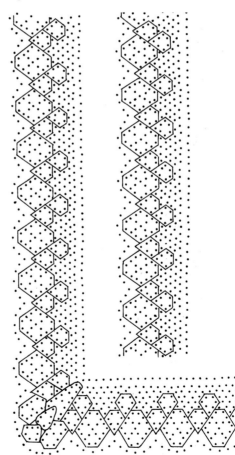

Fig. 277

PATTERN 6

Figs 278, 279 and 280. It is necessary to use a
Coton Perlé no. 8 as the gimp creates the
design and interest.

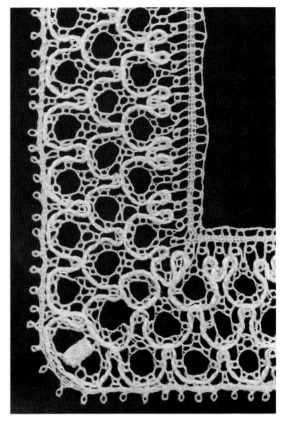

Fig. 278

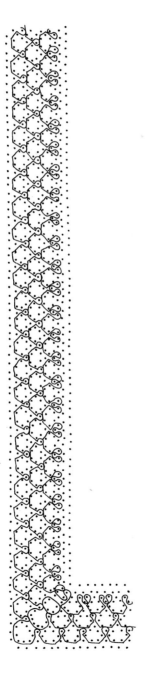

Fig. 280

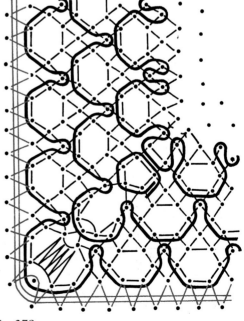

Fig. 279

PATTERN 7

Figs 281 and 282. A geometric pattern. Any corner prepared for this edging rarely looks attractive. It is important to keep the gimp threads tightly wound around the four pin honeycomb buds and Coton Perlé no. 8 is recommended.

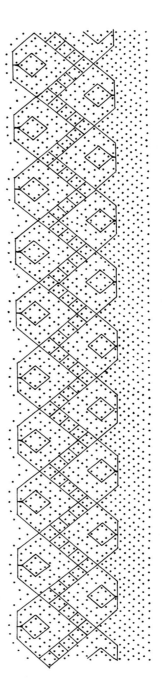

Fig. 282

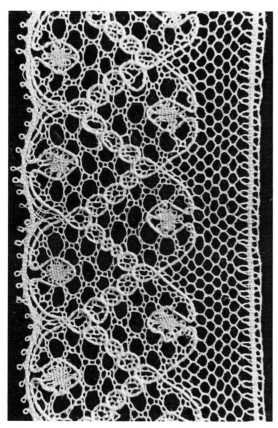

Fig. 281

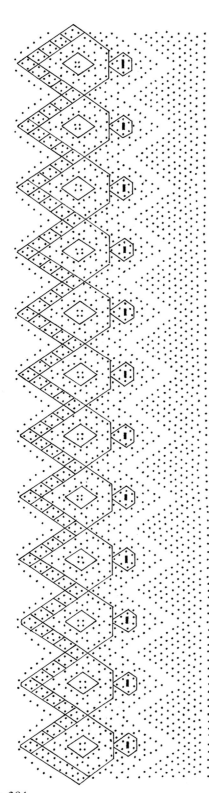

Fig. 284

PATTERN 8

Figs 283 and 284. The passive pairs in the cloth stitch trail should be pulled firmly for a good result. The diamond marked on the pricking indicates an area of cloth stitch, it does not require the use of gimp thread.

Four pin hole in cloth Fig. 285. The weaver works to m, n, o and is supported by pin p. The centre pair is supported by pin z and becomes the weaver for the remaining cloth stitch.

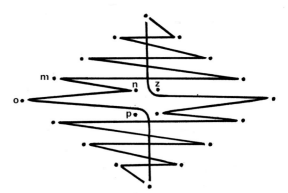

Fig. 285

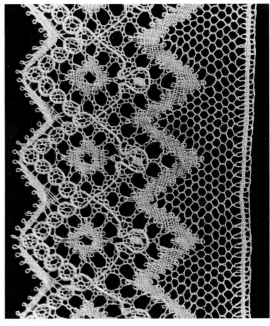

Fig. 283

PATTERN 9

Figs 286 and 287. Two pairs and one single gimp are required.

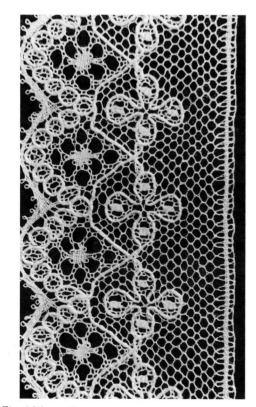

Fig. 286

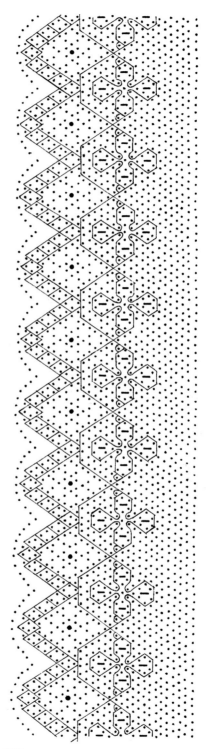

Fig. 287

PATTERN 10

Figs 288 and 289. This pattern is easier to
work than patterns 11 and 12 and is a good
introduction to floral or free Bucks Point lace.

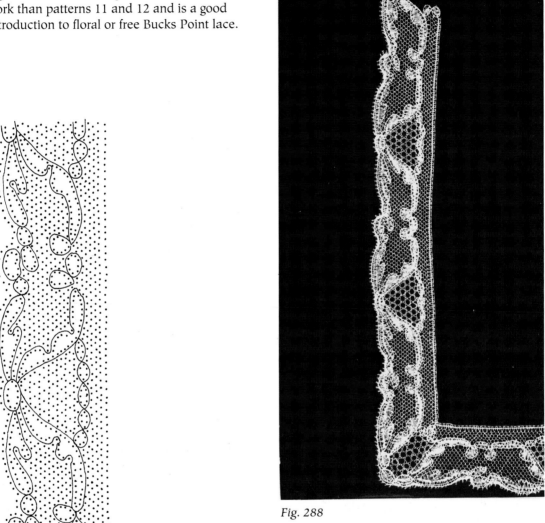

Fig. 288

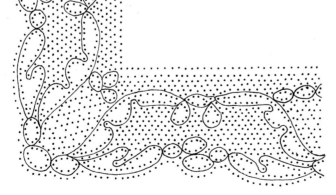

Fig. 289

PATTERN 11

Figs 290 and 291. The circles in the leaves are holes in cloth. The mayflower in the filling is similar to the diagram on page 147. Two consecutive honeycomb stitches are made with the same pairs, this is pin chain.

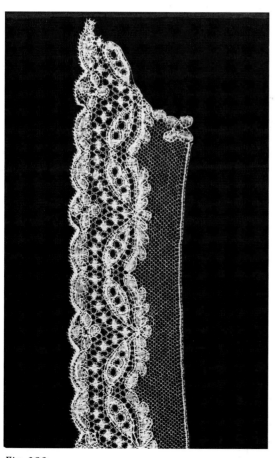

Fig. 290

Fig. 291

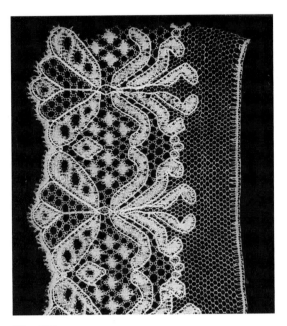

Fig. 292

PATTERN 12

Figs 292 and 293. Make a diagram to plan the use of gimp before beginning the lace. Note that honeycomb and ground are worked diagonally across the corner.

Fig. 293

5. *Joining and Mounting*

The ultimate pleasure in lace making is to achieve a finished article. The time required to join the lace and to mount it should not be underestimated.

Joining lace

There is no merit in making an invisible join unless the lace will withstand wear and laundering. A neat line across the lace is acceptable and rarely noticed as one looks at the whole and not a small portion of the work. Lace mounted permanently within a frame will be discussed later as appearance takes priority and strength is unimportant.

In the past, as lace was made as a continuous edging, two cut ends had to be joined together. It was usual to overlap the lace for one repeat, fold the raw edges inside and oversew. Wider laces with large repeat patterns were joined using a flat seam. The obvious disadvantage – the noticeable thickness – usually disappeared in the fullness of gathering. Today it is still used. For example the lace on a christening gown, whether gathered or not, can be overlapped for strength and will not attract attention. The present demand for corners for Bucks Point handkerchief edgings creates two problems: the difficulty in working the corner

and the problem of achieving a good join when using fine thread.

Until the lacemaker has an understanding of each type of lace, the recommended position and instructions for starting should be followed. However, the more experienced lacemaker should bear in mind the joining when selecting a place to begin. In any pattern it is easier to join into cloth or half stitch features rather than ground or plaits. A gimp thread also helps to make a join less visible.

To make the join Place the beginning of the lace on to the pricking and insert the pins into the correct holes and push them in until the heads are flat on the pillow. Cover with a piece of acetate. The acetate prevents the threads catching in the pins and allows the worker to see the work. Complete the lace until all holes are worked. Press the pins down.

Fig. 294. It is necessary to use a fine hook or a long thin needle with the pointed end fixed into a thin wooden handle. The latter is available from lace suppliers and is often known as a 'lazy Susan'. A hook is put directly through the hole, and one thread pulled through. When using the 'lazy Susan' thread with a piece of cotton 45 cm (18 in) long. A coloured cotton shows more easily but it must not leave fluff which will discolour the lace.

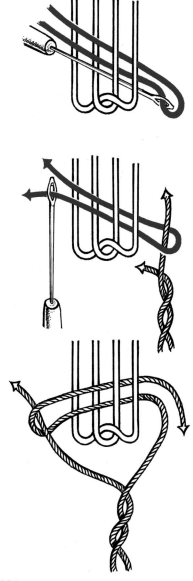

Fig. 294

either end. Use the long thread to oversew the others to cloth or gimp thread. Gradually discard the threads so that the 'cord' of threads does not become too thick.

This method can be used for Torchon, Bedfordshire and Bucks Point laces. Sometimes it is necessary to join plaits into a plait crossing. The thread can be hooked through and knotted as described above. The ends can be oversewn into the original plait or the threads may continue as a plait which lies alongside the original plait or under a leaf to be sewn into the next convenient part of the lace.

Mounting lace on fabric

Fabric and lace should match in texture and fibre. Similarity between the cloth in the lace and the woven fabric is a good guide as to compatability. The colour or shade needs consideration and it is advisable to purchase thread and fabric before starting the project. The width of hem and lace should be in proportion. Practice is worthwhile to check stitch size and the chosen thread for mounting. Lace thread may be the most suitable.

There are two basic methods:

1   Lace attached directly on to the fabric. Is the lace to be permanently sewn to one piece of fabric? Or is this an occasion when a narrow beading is placed between lace and fabric (so that the lace can be attached temporarily)? This can be made very quickly with the same lace thread.
2   The fabric neatened with a hem or buttonhole stitch and the lace attached later.

Reference to specialized books on mounting lace or embroidery stitches is suggested. Two methods are described below.

1   THREE-SIDED STITCH

The lace is mounted directly on to the fabric.

Figs 295 and 296 illustrate diagrammatic working of the stitch, but it is important to use

Take a pair of bobbins from the completed lace to the correct position at the beginning of the lace. Ascertain that any necessary twists are present, remove the pin and pull one thread through the hole as a loop. Remove the coloured thread. Pass the other thread from the same pair through and pull both ends tightly, tie with a reef knot. Join all threads in similarly. Cut off the bobbins, leaving 4 inches (100 mm) of thread but a longer thread at

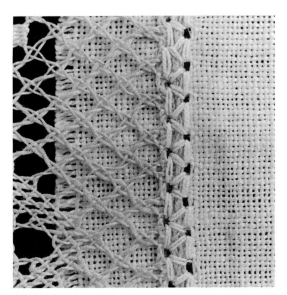

Fig. 295

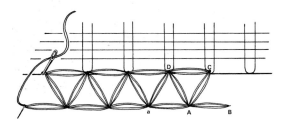

Fig. 296

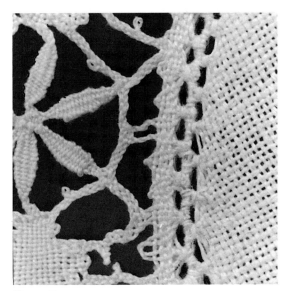

Fig. 297

a sewing needle with a *large eye* (crewel nee-dle) and to pull the stitches *very tightly* to make the double row of holes.

Work as follows on the right side of the fabric:

Bring the needle out at A.

Put the needle in at B and out at A
    (back stitch).

Put the needle in at B and out at A
    (back stitch).

Put the needle in at C and out at A.

Put the needle in at C and out at D.

Put the needle in at C and out at D.

Put the needle in at C and out at D.

Put the needle in at A and out at D.

Put the needle in at A and out at a.

Fig. 297 illustrates the finished work. The problem that arises is the neat and strong neatening of the fabric on the wrong side. It is usual to overcast the raw edge and then cut

the remaining fabric away. However, to facili-tate this and prevent fraying it is suggested that a narrow line of zigzag stitches is made using a sewing machine before the lace is tacked on to the fabric. This should be about five threads outside the position of the edge of the lace. This may not be acceptable if lace is entered in competitions where the entire work should be hand done. This method is suitable for lace on a curved edge. Alternatively, on a straight line the lace can be attached with three-sided stitch brought to the edge and the fabric folded on to the wrong side. This should be tacked very firmly using a tacking stitch at right angles to the edge. Three-sided stitch is worked to cover the raw edge and hold the hem in position. Referring back to Fig. 296 – A and B on single fabric and C and D on double fabric. Figs 298a and 298b illustrate the right and wrong side of the finished work. The stitching may be worked from right or wrong side, but if from the wrong side extra stitches are needed on the diagonal to retain the appearance of double stitches throughout. This is suitable for coarse fabrics.

2   PIN STITCH

This is useful to neaten hems when the fabric is too fine to draw threads. It is also used as a

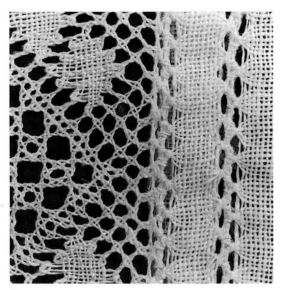

Fig. 298a

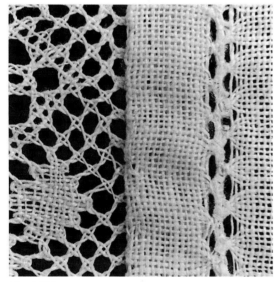

Fig. 298b

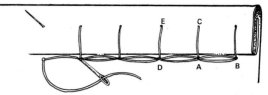

Fig. 299

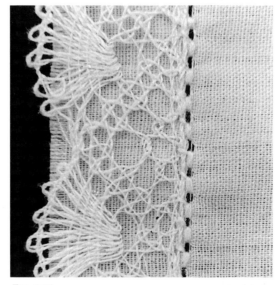

Fig. 300

*Put the needle in at A and out at D.
Put the needle in at A and out at D.
Put the needle in at A and out at E*.
Repeat from * to * for the length required. Fig. 300 shows the stitch when lace is mounted directly on to fabric.

1   A neat hem is made and the lace is invisibly stitched on to the edge. This is particularly useful for handkerchiefs and fine fabrics. Figs 301a and 301b show right and wrong sides.
The corners should be mitred. Refer to Fig. 302. Using the fabric threads, ascertain that the corner is square, and fold it so that the raw edges (A) are together. Line B is the fold of the hem and C the edge of the finished article. The line ab is at right angles to the diagonal fold line, back stitch from a to b. Cut away surplus fabric on line zz 1/8th in (4 mm) from ab. Turn through and prepare the hem and other corners.

method for attaching lace directly on to fabric, although it is difficult to ensure that the lace will not pull away when the excess fabric has been cut away.
To work the stitch, Fig. 299 shows the work in diagrammatic form. Again use a crewel needle and pull the stitches tightly.
Bring the needle out at A.
Put the needle in at B and out at A.
Put the needle in at B and out at C.

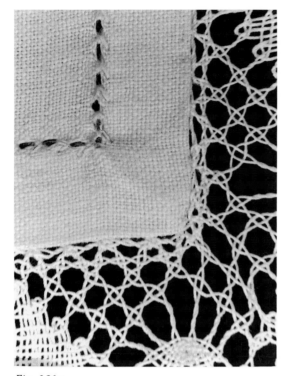

Fig. 301a

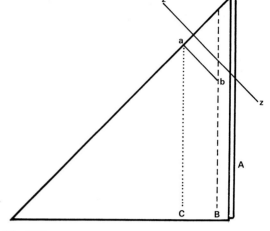

Fig. 302

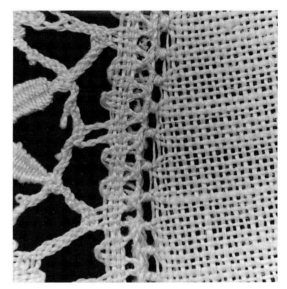

Fig. 303

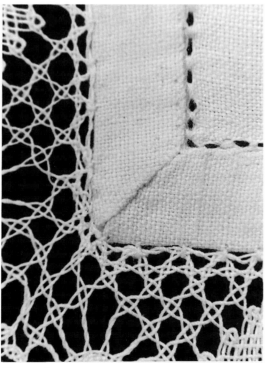

Fig. 301b

2 The lace is attached directly to the fabric with pin stitch, it is sometimes used on a curved edge (Fig. 303) but it is difficult to leave sufficient fabric to withstand wear. The vertical stitch passes through the lace and the back stitches are in the fabric close to the edge of the lace. The fabric must be cut away behind the lace and the raw edges overcast. This is only satisfactory when there are two or three passive pairs in the lace which will hide the overcast edge. Fig. 304a illustrates the use of pin stitch on a diago-

Fig. 304a

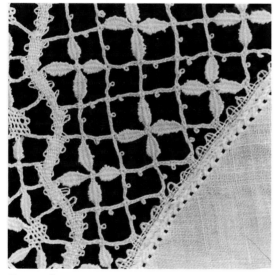

Fig. 304b

to ensure the mounted lace does not touch the glass. It should be in keeping with the lace, a heavy wooden frame is rarely suitable for a very fine work. The piece of lace must be in proportion to the margin surrounding it and generally the more dense the lace appears, the greater the margin required.

Complete the lace and when appropriate join with knots. The mounting fabric is not cut to size until the lace is in position. Thread the ends of lace thread through to the wrong side of the fabric and when the appearance is satisfactory knot them in pairs. Place a piece of iron-on interfacing over the ends and seal them in. The fabric is ready to be cut to size. If the fabric is loosely woven or frays easily, iron a piece of interfacing on before attaching the lace.

Bookmarks and Samplers

These may be sewn with very small stitches on to a piece of ribbon. However, unless they are to be used on one occasion only they become discoloured and the appearance deteriorates. It is possible to purchase plastic covers from lace suppliers, but it is essential to check the width before making the lace.

nal handkerchief corner. Fig. 304b shows the wrong side and overcast raw edges.

Mounting in frames

The pattern, thread, backing fabric and frame should be brought together before starting the project. A frame should have sufficient depth

Appendix

These can be enlarged or reduced using a photocopier.

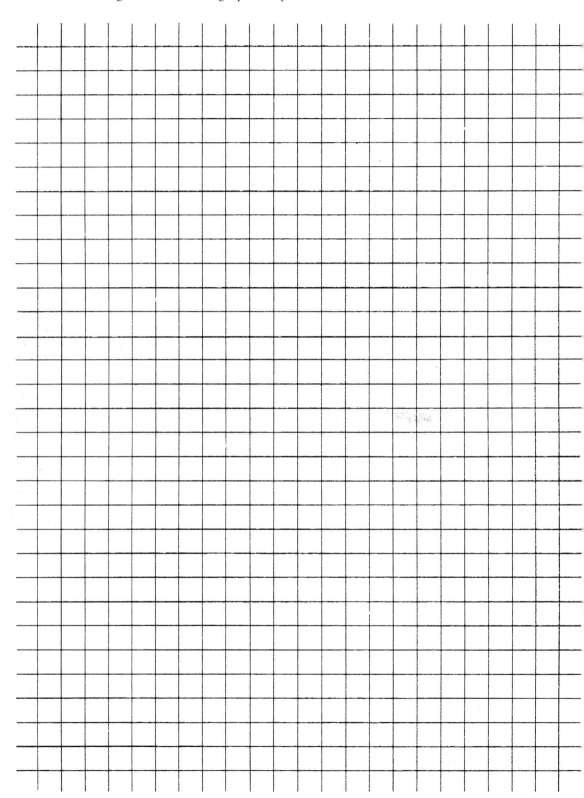

A   45° grid for Torchon prickings

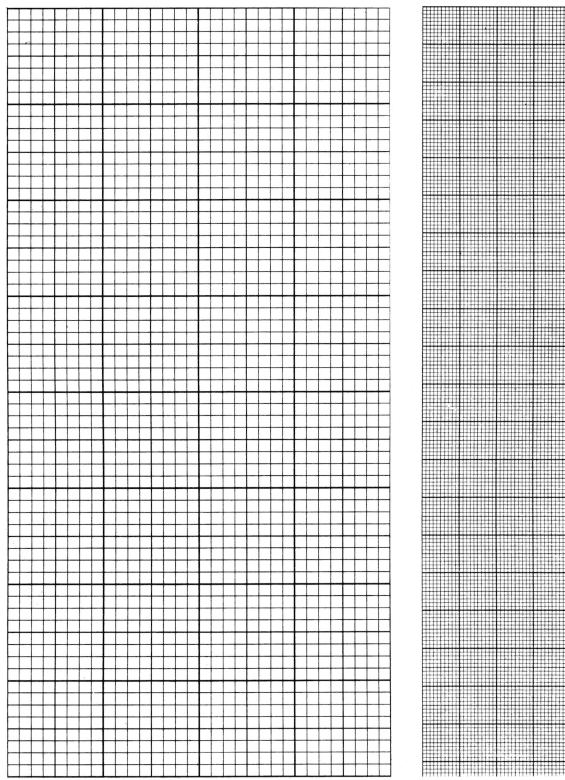

B   55° grid for Bucks Point prickings

C   60° grid for Bucks
Point prickings

Sources of Information

United Kingdom

OIDFA
Jean Barratt
71 The Oval
Brookfield
Middlesborough TS5 8EZ

The Lace Guild
The Hollies
53 Audnam
Stourbridge
West Midlands DY8 4AE

The Lacemakers' Circle
49 Wardwick
Derby DE1 1HY

The Lace Society
Linwood
Stratford Road
Oversley
Alcester
War BY9 6PG

The British College of Lace
21 Hillmorton Road
Rugby
War CV22 5DF

Ring of Tatters
Miss B. Netherwood
269 Oregon Way
Chaddesden
Derby DE21 6UR

United Kingdom Director of
International Old Lacers
S. Hurst
4 Dollis Road
London N3 1RG

Belgium

OIDFA/Belgische
Kantorganisatie
Lydia Thiels-Mertens
Jagersberg 1
B-3294 Molenstede-Diest

France

OIDFA
Suzanne Puech
3 Chemin de Parenty
F-69250 Neuville sur Saône

Germany

OIDFA
Uta Ulrich
Papenbergweg 33
D-4930 Detmold

Deutscher Klöppelverband
e. V.
Ortolanweg 7
D-1000 Berlin 47

The Netherlands

OIDFA
Puck Smelter-Hoekstra
Corona 68
NL-3204 CM Spijkenisse

LOKK
Boterbloem 56
NL-7322 GX Apeldoorn

Switzerland

FDS
(Fédération de Dentellières
Suisses)
Evelyne Lütolf
Buhnstrasse 12
CH-8052 Zürich

USA

OIDFA
Kathy Kauffmann
1301 Greenwood
Wilmette
Illinois 60091

International Old Lacers
124 West Irvington Place
Denver
CO 80223-1539

Lace & Crafts magazine
3201 East Lakeshore Drive
Tallahassee
FL 32312-2034

Equipment Suppliers

England

BEDFORDSHIRE
A. Sells
49 Pedley Lane
Clifton
Shefford SG17 5QT

BERKSHIRE
Chrisken Bobbins
26 Cedar Drive
Kingsclere RG15 8TD

BUCKINGHAMSHIRE
J. S. Sear
Lacecraft Supplies
8 Hillview
Sherington MK16 9NJ

Winslow Bobbins
70 Magpie Way
Winslow MK18 3PZ
SMP

4 Garners Close
Chalfont St Peter SL9
    0HB

CAMBRIDGESHIRE
Josie and Jeff Harrison
Walnut Cottage
Winwick
Huntingdon PE17 5PP

Heffers Graphic Shop
    (*matt
    coloured transparent
    adhesive film*)
26 King Street
Cambridge CB1 1LN

Spangles
Carole Morris
Cashburn lane
Burwell CB5 0ED

CHESHIRE
Lynn Turner
Church Meadow Crafts
7 Woodford Road
Winsford

DEVON
Honiton Lace Shop
44 High Street
Honiton EX14 8PJ

DORSET
Frank Herring & Sons
27 High West Street
Dorchester DT1 1UP

T. Parker (*mail order,
    general and bobbins*)
124 Corhampton Road
Boscombe East
Bournemouth BH6 5NZ

ESSEX
Needlework
Ann Bartleet
Bucklers Farm
Coggeshall CO6 1SB

GLOUCESTERSHIRE
T. Brown (*pillows*)
Temple Lane Cottage
Littledean
Cinderford

Chosen Crafts Centre
46 Winchcombe Street
Cheltenham GL2 2ND

HAMPSHIRE
Needlestyle
24_26 West Street
Alresford

Richard Viney (*bobbins*)
Unit 7
Port Royal Street
Southsea PO5 3UD

ISLE OF WIGHT
Busy Bobbins
Unit 7
Scarrots Lane
Newport PO30 1JD

KENT
The Handicraft Shop
47 Northgagte
Canterbury CT1 1BE

Denis Hornsby
25 Manwood Avenue
Canterbury CT2 7AH

Francis Iles
73 High Street
Rochester ME1 1LX

LANCASHIRE
Malcolm J. Fielding
    (*bobbins*)
2 Northern Terrace
Moss Lane
Silverdale LA5 0ST

LINCOLNSHIRE
Ken and Pat Schultz
Whynacres
Shepeau Stow
Whaplode Drove
Spalding PE12 0TU

MERSEYSIDE
Hayes & Finch
Head Office & Factory
Hanson Road
Aintree
Liverpool L9 9BP

MIDDLESEX
Redburn Crafts
Squires Garden Centre
Halliford Road
Upper Halliford
Shepperton TW17 8RU

NORFOLK
Stitches and Lace
Alby Craft Centre
Cromer Road
Alby
Norwich NR11 7QE

Jane's Pincushions
Taverham Craft Unit 4
Taverham Nursery
 Centre
Fir Covert Road
Taverham
Norwich NR8 6HT

George Walker
The Corner Shop
Rickinghall, Diss

NORTH HUMBERSIDE
Teazle Embroideries
35 Boothferry Road
Hull

NORTH YORKSHIRE
The Craft House
23 Bar Street
Scarborough
Stitchery
Finkle Street
Richmond

SOUTH YORKSHIRE
D. H. Shaw
47 Lamor Crescent
Thrushcroft
Rotherham S66 9QD

STAFFORDSHIRE
J. & J. Ford (mail order
 and lace days only)
October Hill
Upper Way
Upper Longdon
Rugeley WS15 1QB

SUFFOLK
A. R. Archer (bobbins)
The Poplars
Shetland
near Stowmarket IP14
 3DE

Mary Collins (*linen by
 the metre, and made
 up articles of church
 linen*)
Church Furnishings
St Andrews Hall
Humber Doucy Lane
Ipswich IP4 3BP

E. & J. Piper (*silk
 embroidery
 and lace thread*)
Silverlea
Flax Lane
Glemsford CO10 7RS

SURREY
Needle and Thread
80 High Street
Horsell
Woking GU21 4SZ

Needlestyle
5 The Woolmead
Farnham GU9 7TX

SUSSEX
Southern Handicrafts
20 Kensington Gardens
Brighton BN1 4AC

WARWICKSHIRE
Christine & David
 Springett
21 Hillmorton Road
Rugby CV22 5DF

WEST MIDLANDS
Framecraft
83 Hampstead Road
Handsworth Wood
Birmingham B2 1JA

The Needlewoman
21 Needles Alley
off New Street
Birmingham B2 5AE

Stitches
Dovehouse Shopping
 Parade
Warwick Road
Olton, Solihull

WEST YORKSHIRE
Jo Firth
*Lace marketing &
 Needlecraft Supplies*
58 Kent Crescent
Lowtown
Pudsey LS28 9EB

Just Lace
Lacemaker Supplies
14 Ashwood Gardens
Gildersome
Leeds LS27 7AS

Sebalace
Waterloo Mills
Howden Road
Silsden BD20 0HA

George White
 Lacemaking
 Supplies
40 Heath Drive
Boston Spa LS23 6PB

WILTSHIRE
Doreen Campbell
 (*frames and mounts*)
Highcliff
Bremilham Road
Malmesbury SN16 0DQ

Scotland

Christine Riley
53 Barclay Street
Stonehaven
Kincardineshire

Peter & Beverley
 Scarlett
Strupak
Hill Head
Cold Wells, Ellon
Grampian

Wales

Bryncraft Bobbins
B. J. Phillips
Pantglas
Cellan
Lampeter
Dyfed SA48 8JD

Hilkar Lace Suppliers
33 Mysydd Road
Landore
Swansea

Australia

*Australian Lace
 Magazine*
P.O. Box 609
Manly
NSW 2095

Dentelles Lace Supplies
c/o Betty Franks
39 Lang Terrace
Northgate 4013
Brisbane
Queensland

The Lacemaker
724a Riversdale Road
Camberwell
Victoria 3124

Spindle and Loom
83 Longueville Road
Lane Cove
NSW 2066

Tulis Crafts
201 Avoca Street
Randwick
NSW 2031

Belgium

't Handwerkhuisje
Katelijnestraat 23
8000 Bruges

Kantcentrum
Balstraat 14
8000 Bruges

Manufacture Belge de
   Dentelle
6 Galerie de la Reine
Galeries Royales St
   Hubert
1000 Bruxelles

Orchidée
Mariastraat 18
8000 Bruges

Ann Thys
't Apostelientje
Balstraat 11
8000 Bruges

France

Centre d'Enseignement
   à la
   Dentelle du Puy
2 Rue Duguesclin
43000 Le Puy en Velay

A L'Econome
Anne-Marie Deydier
Ecole de Dentelle aux
   Fuseaux
10 rue Paul Chenavard
69001 Lyon

Rougier and Plé
13_15 Bd des Filles de
   Calvaire
75003 Paris

Germany

Barbara Fay
Verlag &
   Versandbuchhandlun
   g
Am Goosberg 2
D-W 2330 Gammelby

P. P. Hempel
Ortolanweg 34
1000 Berlin

Holland

Blokker's Boektiek
Bronsteeweg 4/4a
2101 AC Heemstede

Theo Brejaart
Dordtselaan 146_148
PO Box 5199
3008 AD Rotterdam

Heikina de Rüyter
Zuiderstraat 1
9693 ER Nieweschans

Magazijn *De Vlijt*
Lijnmarkt 48
Utrecht

Netherlands

Tiny van Donschor
Postbus 482
6000 A1 Weert

Switzerland

Buchhandlung
Dr A. Scheidegger & Co.
   AG
Obere Bahnhofstr. 10A
CH-8901 Affoltern a.A.

Martin Burkhard
Klöppelzubehör
Jurastrasse 7
CH-5300 Turgi

Fadehax
Inh. Irene Solca
4105 Biel-Benken
Basel

New Zealand

Peter McLeavey
P.O. Box 69.007
Auckland 8

USA

Arbor House
22 Arbor Lane
Roslyn Heights
NY 11577

Baltazor Inc.
3262 Severn Avenue
Metairie
LA 7002

Beggars' Lace
P.O. Box 481223
Denver
Colo 80248

Berga Ullman Inc.
P.O. Box 918
North Adams
MA 01247

Happy Hands
3007 S. W. Marshall
Pendleton
Oreg 97180

International Old
   Lacers Inc.
124 West Irvington
   Place
Denver
CO 80223-1539

The Lacemaker
23732-G Bothell Hwy,
   SE
Bothell
WA 98021

Lace Place de Belgique
800 S. W. 17th Street
Boca Raton
FL 33432

Lacis
3163 Adeline Street
Berkeley
CA 94703

Robin's Bobbins
RT1 Box 1736
Mineral Bluff
GA 30559-9736

Robin and Russ
Handweavers
533 North Adams Street
McMinnville
Oreg 97128

The Unique And Art
   Lace
   Cleaners
5926 Delman
   Boulevard
St Louis
MO 63112

Unicorn Books
Glimakra Looms 'n
   Yarns Inc.
1304 Scott Street
Petaluma
CA 94954-1181

Van Sciver Bobbin Lace
130 Cascadilla Park
Ithaca
NY 14850

The World in Stitches
82 South Street
Milford
N.H. 03055

Index